SPECIAL NEEDS in the primary years

The essential A–Z guide to special needs

INFORMATION ON TERMS AND CONDITIONS • HOW YOU CAN HELP • WHERE TO GO TO FIND OUT MORE

DR HANNAH MORTIMER

Author
Dr Hannah Mortimer

Editor
Victoria Lee

Assistant Editors
Jane Gartside/Aileen Lalor

Series Designers
Sarah Rock/Anna Oliwa

Designer
Andrea Lewis

Illustrations
Debbie Clark

Cover artwork
Richard Johnson

Acknowledgements
Disability Equality in Education for the use of material based on a Venn diagram from
Inclusion in the early years: DEE Course Book by Richard Rieser and Christine O'Mahony ©
Richard Rieser and Christine O'Mahony (2001, Disability Equality in Education)

Every effort has been made to trace copyright holders and the publishers apologise for any
inadvertent omissions.

Text © 2004, Hannah Mortimer
© 2004, Scholastic Ltd

Designed using Adobe InDesign

Published by Scholastic Ltd, Villiers House,
Clarendon Avenue, Leamington Spa, Warwickshire CV32 5PR

Visit our website at www.scholastic.co.uk

Printed by Bell & Bain Ltd, Glasgow

2 3 4 5 6 7 8 9 0   5 6 7 8 9 0 1 2 3

British Library Cataloguing-in-Publication Data A catalogue record for this book is
available from the British Library.

ISBN 0 439 97162 4

The essential A–Z guide to special needs

CONTENTS · CONTENTS · CONTENTS · CONTENTS · CONTENTS

INTRODUCTION
Class teachers have the responsibility of meeting any special educational needs in their classes. This book provides the basic information needed to fulfil this.

The aims of the series

There is a revised *Code of Practice* in England for the identification and assessment of special educational needs that has been published by the DfES. This gives new guidance on including children who have disabilities. In addition, the QCA Schemes of Work and the National Numeracy and National Literacy Strategies emphasise the key role that teachers play in making sure that the curriculum is accessible to all pupils. This series aims to provide suggestions to class teachers and others working in schools on how to meet and monitor special educational needs (SEN) under the new guidelines. It will provide accessible information and advice for class teachers and subject teachers at KS1 and KS2. It will also provide practical examples in the activity books of how they can use this information to plan inclusive teaching across all areas of the National Curriculum.

There is related legislation and guidance in Wales, Scotland and Northern Ireland though the detail and terminology is different. For example, the 'statement' of SEN in England and Wales is called a 'Record' in Scotland. Nevertheless, the general approaches and information covered in this book will be relevant throughout the UK.

Who this book is for

First and foremost, this book is for class teachers and support assistants who work on a daily basis with the children. It will provide staff with their first point of reference for understanding SEN and will be helpful to have close at hand in a busy classroom. Each school is required to appoint a special educational needs co-ordinator (SENCO) who will act as the contact point for all SEN matters. The book will also be helpful for SENCOs, headteachers and governors to use with the staff they work with.

The SENCO's role is to support their colleagues in meeting SEN in their schools though it is the responsibility of *each staff member* to support children who have SEN within their classes. This complete guide will help in the provision of general information needed about conditions, terms, issues and guidelines, all in one place for easy reference. SENCOs are busy people and cannot always be present when a member of staff needs quick and basic information. This book can serve as a starting point for staff, who can then contact the SENCO for further information and detail as needed, leaning on the other books in this series and particularly the *Special Needs Handbook*. Many SENCOs are also taking on a new role in ensuring Equal Opportunities within their

schools and this book contains basic information that will support this additional role. Finally, the book will also be a useful reference for parents, carers, and trainees.

How to use this book

You are not expected to be an expert on SEN. You already have an expertise in individual children, how they learn, their strengths and their weaknesses. This book provides you with the very basics so that you can be familiar enough with the terminology and issues to be able to ask the right questions and talk confidently with parents and carers. The book covers 54 frequently used terms, approaches or conditions associated with SEN, arranged in alphabetical order and each one on a separate page. You can dip into the book for quick reference, or you can skim through these easy-to-read pages to provide yourself with a basic level of knowledge.

On each page, you will find a few basic facts that will be helpful for you to know. There might be a definition of a term or a description of a condition. This is followed by a section on 'how to help' that lists the essentials of what it actually means for you and your practice. There is a section on working with parents and on making links with other professionals or agencies involved. There are also pointers for 'finding out more', either from an organisation or through reading more about the subject. At the end of the book, there is a list of useful contacts including voluntary organisations and suppliers of resources. You will find further lists in the other books within the 'Special needs in the primary years' series.

The SEN Code of Practice

All schools are required to 'have regard to' the Code of Practice. This is a guide for school governors, schools and LEAs about the practical help they can give to children with special educational needs. It recommends that schools should identify children's needs and take action to meet them as early as possible, working with parents. The aim is to enable all pupils to reach their full potential, to be included fully in school communities and to make a successful transition to adulthood. The Code gives guidance to schools but does not tell them what they must do in every case.

Support systems

It is recognised that good practice can take many forms and schools are encouraged to adopt a flexible and a graduated response to the SEN of individual children. This approach recognises that there is a continuum of SEN and, where necessary, brings increasing specialist expertise on board if the child is experiencing continuing difficulties. Once a child's SEN have been identified, providers should intervene through 'School Action' or 'School Action Plus'. About one in six children might be expected to have SEN at some stage in their school career and some may require special action to be taken at one point in their schooling and then no longer need it at another. Only about two in a hundred pupils receive a 'statement' of SEN and this figure is decreasing as more support becomes delegated to

schools. Each maintained school now has a budget for meeting the SEN of the pupils, which should be earmarked for those children. However, *special support* need not mean *individual help* and that budget should be used in a flexible way to make sure a child with SEN is included in the curriculum as far as possible and not segregated or excluded.

Parents and carers of children with SEN now have stronger rights and most LEAs appoint Parent Partnership Officers to offer advice and to support parents at any stage of the SEN process. These professionals work alongside schools and support services but are also able to give independent advice. They can listen to parents' worries and concerns, explain the statutory assessment processes to them and help them have their say or develop their input.

Developing inclusive practice

Inclusion is the practice of including all children in a school. All children participate fully in all the regular routines and activities of the classroom and school day though these might need to be modified to meet individual children's goals and teaching targets. There seem to be certain common features that promote inclusion.

● There is usually careful joint planning. For example, if there is special support for a child, how will it be used? Will the child still have access to the full range of adults, children and activities?

● Staff use educational labels rather than categories or medical labels (such as 'a child who has epilepsy' rather than 'an epileptic' or ' a child who has SEN' rather than 'an SEN child').

● School staff provide good role models for the children through positive expectations and the way they respect and value the children.

● Special attention is given to improving children's access and communication skills.

● Teaching strategies are developed which enable *all* children to participate and to learn.

● Individual approaches are planned which draw on pupils' experiences, set high expectations and encourage peer support.

● There is a flexible use of support to promote joining in and inclusion rather than to create barriers and exclusion.

Flexible approaches

In an inclusive approach, your task becomes one of making the National Curriculum accessible to all. The two main ways in which you can set out to achieve this is by making sure that the curriculum you offer is both *inclusive* and *differentiated*. You can read about this in more detail in the *Special Needs Handbook* from this series. Having 'special' activities for 'special' children and buying plenty of 'special needs' equipment does not help the development of inclusive services. So often, an activity can be changed in some way rather than excluding certain children from it because they cannot 'fit in' with it. Flexible approaches and adaptable timetables and routines make this easier. The management guide *Including all children in the literacy hour and daily mathematics lesson* (DfES 2002) provides guidelines on how you can cater for pupils with particular needs

including SEN and how best to use classroom assistants. If you combine that general guidance with the specific tips in this book, you will have a starting point for addressing and meeting the needs of most SEN you are likely to come across in your class. Your role is not to *solve* special educational needs but to *identify them*, *plan for them* and *meet them*. If you find that the child is still not making reasonable progress despite your interventions, then you can consult the SENCO and make use of the SEN Code of Practice.

Thinking ahead

If you are going to include a wide range of SEN within your class, outdoor play and learning areas need to contain quiet, sheltered spaces as well as busy, active areas. Indoors, tables and equipment need to be at adjustable heights and floor spaces comfortable and safe to work and play on. Acoustics can be softened with soft surfaces, cushions, carpets and curtains, making it easier for everyone to hear clearly. Group times can be kept concrete by using props and visual aids. Communication can be enhanced by making sure that all adults are familiar with any language or communication system used by the children. Children can also have a communication book showing how they make their needs known. Making more use of colours, textures and smells can encourage the use, development and expression of different senses. Colleagues can look for ways of making their tools and equipment easy to handle by all children. Throughout the curriculum, you can look out for materials, pictures and books that portray positive images of disabled people and special needs.

There is an overlap between disability, special educational needs and significant medical difficulties, and this is why you will find pages on all of these. Not all children who are disabled or who have a medical condition will have special educational needs. However, it is helpful if you can understand all of these conditions so that you can make sure each child is fully included in your school.

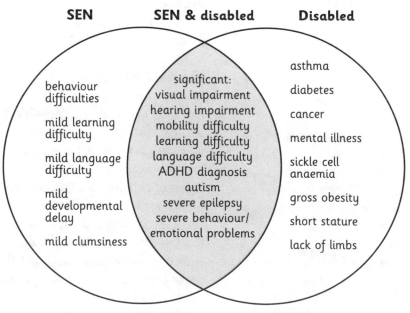

Aggression

What you need to know
- Some children find it hard to mix with other children without becoming physical with them. There are many different reasons for this and you cannot make assumptions.
- Sometimes these children might catch your eye first before attacking another child, suggesting that they are seeking attention.
- Others might seem constantly angry or frustrated because they find it hard to speak clearly, to communicate effectively, to understand or to hear. These children become quickly defensive and this can lead to aggression.
- Others still enjoy physical play at break-times but tend to become over boisterous and aggressive, perhaps because they are acting out a favourite but violent TV series, film or computer game.
- For other children, the aggressive behaviour might be linked to their home experiences or to past events in their lives. Perhaps an over-physical approach is a way of life for them.
- There are also some children who would love to make friends but who lack social skills and end up being too physical

How to help
- Sit down with colleagues and decide what you mean when you say the child is being aggressive. What is the child actually doing?
- Decide why you feel a child is being aggressive. You can do this by observing the child carefully.
- Either try a 'fly-on-the-wall' observation where you record what the child does over an hour or so. Ask colleagues to deal with all incidents in their usual way so that other children are protected.
- Alternatively, use an 'ABC' chart, recording difficult times by listing what led to the incident (antecedent), what the child did (behaviour), and what happened as a result (consequence).
- You can then plan an intervention that involves changing the antecedent or the consequences and make sure that all your colleagues follow the same approach. This might involve avoiding certain difficult times, perhaps by making sure that an adult works or plays near the child whenever a certain other child is present or providing a distraction or alternative activity at break-times.
- You will need to give short, clear rules and intervene with consistency. This can be difficult when there are various adults dealing with the child. You might find it easiest to be consistent in your approaches if other adults refer all incidents to you for a while.
- Work hard to ensure that the child develops confidence and competence in other aspects of school life.

Finding out more
Plans for Better Behaviour in the Primary School by Sue Roffey and Terry O'Reirdan (David Fulton).

WORKING WITH CARERS
- Talk with parents and carers about whether the child's behaviour is the same at home. What do they do that helps? Develop a style of language that refers to the *behaviour* as the problem and not the child or the family. That way, you can plan approaches without ascribing blame.

MAKING LINKS
- Find out from the LEA who your Behaviour Support Teacher is for general advice and training. See also the pages on Behaviour Difficulties (page 12) for a behaviour management approach and AD/HD (page 13), since these children might also display aggressive behaviour.

Allergy

What you need to know

● Some children's bodies react to certain substances by producing a rash, runny eyes and nose, or developing breathing difficulties or changed behaviour. This is due to an altered immune response called an allergic reaction.

● Children react to a wide range of different substances. They might be things a child has inhaled, touched or otherwise taken into their bodies, such as pollen, dust mites, animals, penicillin, nuts, foods, latex or certain chemicals.

● An allergic condition can be very mild or extremely serious and life threatening, such as when a child goes into anaphylactic shock and medical help is needed immediately. It will depend on each child and the particular reaction they produce in response to the allergen.

● Allergic reactions might be delayed or might develop very quickly and obviously.

● These children are not infectious and an allergy cannot be 'caught'.

How to help

● Ask parents/carers routinely about any allergies their child has when he or she first joins you.

● Find out what this means for the child and for you. How serious is the reaction? What are the signs you should look out for and at what stage should you take any special action? What foods or situations should be avoided? Look for a 'common sense' balance in keeping school experiences as normal as possible yet taking reasonable precautions to ensure that the child remains comfortable and safe.

● If a child has a serious allergic reaction, mount a reminder to all staff on the staffroom wall stating what the child's allergy is, what to avoid, what to look out for, what constitutes an emergency and what action to take.

● Keep an eye on the environment outside your classroom so that you can close windows if the traffic pollution is particularly bad or the pollen count high.

● If a child is very uncomfortable, stay calm, reassure and distract them while you take any necessary action.

● Make sure that you are absolutely certain about the ingredients of the food you provide; for some children it is essential that they do not have even the smallest trace of an allergen such as a nut.

● Make sure that the catering staff are given clear and precise information about any food allergies.

● Encourage older children to take some responsibility themselves.

Finding out more

The Anaphylaxis Campaign produces guidance for carers. Send an SAE to PO Box 149, Fleet, Hampshire GU13 9XU or visit www.anaphylaxis.org.uk.

WORKING WITH CARERS

● For children who have marked symptoms, or for those whose allergies are still being assessed, keep a diary to share with parents/carers about what led up to a reaction, what the reaction was, and what happened as a result. This is useful for parents/carers to share with the medical professionals. The same kind of diary system can be used for recording day-to-day reactions for children with known allergies.

MAKING LINKS

● Contact your local health visitor or school nurse for general advice about management of a child's allergies. See also 'Asthma' (page 12) and 'Eczema' (page 28), since both of these can be caused by allergies.

Asperger's Syndrome

What you need to know

● Asperger's Syndrome is a brain dysfunction which leads to a collection or 'syndrome' of unusual behaviours. These are as follows.

- Children with Asperger's Syndrome may appear to behave in an autistic way and yet their language is not usually delayed.
- There is an impairment of two-way social interaction so that they appear to function 'in a world of their own'.
- They have very poor social skills and may wish to make friends but do not know how.
- Their speech may be odd and pedantic, as if they are older than their years, and the content may be centred on topics of intense interest.
- These children may have limited facial expressions and cannot use or understand non-verbal cues such as body posture or gestures.
- They may find change difficult to cope with and enjoy repetitive activities and routines.
- They may have excellent rote memory for topics of interest. They may be physically clumsy as well.

How to help

● Use photographs as visual timetables to show the child the typical routine of the day and refer to it together at each change of activity.
● Early on, teach the skills of asking permission, seeking help, taking a turn or waiting in a line. *Show* the child what to do as well as telling.
● Teach simple turn-taking routines (such as football or number table games) that make another child's company useful and fun. Support the child as the game is played with one other child, then increase the group size.
● Try to explain jokes and humour, as these might be difficult for the child to grasp. Avoid sarcasm at all costs.
● Support the child's interests but introduce new things too.
● Circle time is an excellent way of teaching talking and listening skills, as well getting to know each other.
● Help the child to avoid undue stress, as this will make their autistic features more marked. Provide a quiet corner to withdraw to if the child feels 'overloaded', particularly during unstructured times such as free play, lunch times or breaks.
● Be aware that abstract language might be interpreted very literally and that the child's thinking might be rather 'black and white'.

Finding out more

Asperger Syndrome – A Practical Guide for Teachers by Val Cumine et al (David Fulton). The National Autistic Society provides support and advice for carers and professionals. You can contact them at 393 City Road, London EC1V 1NG, 0870 600 85 85, www.nas.org.uk.

WORKING WITH CARERS

● Convey to parents or carers that you are trying to understand what the syndrome means to their child and therefore, you do not see his or her behaviour as 'naughty'.
● Work out together *why* the child might be behaving in a certain way so that you can help. Parents/carers will usually know their child inside out - never make assumptions!

MAKING LINKS

● Most LEAs now have an Autism Support Team – contact your local educational psychologist or support teacher for information.
● See 'Autistic spectrum difficulties' (page 11) since the conditions overlap.

Asthma

What you need to know
● Asthma causes children to cough, wheeze, have a tight chest and get short of breath. This is because their airways are almost always inflamed and sensitive. These airways react badly when the child has a cold or comes into contact with an asthma 'trigger'.

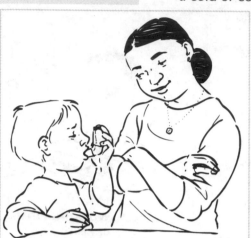

● Common asthma triggers include viral infections, pollen, cigarette smoke, house-dust mites, furry or feathery pets, exercise, air pollution and stress.
● Children whose asthma has been diagnosed by a doctor will need to take a dose of their prescribed reliever medication when they have symptoms. This is usually given by inhaler. Some children need to use a preventer inhaler each day as well.
● Asthma symptoms can be very mild for some children, and extremely severe for others.
● Each school should have guidance on the use of medication in school, who can administer it and what consents are needed from parents/carers and doctors.

How to help
● Keep a diary record for any child who has asthma so that you can identify any triggers in school. Record the child's symptoms and what you think might have set them off.
● Keep any inhaler in a safe place (refer to school guidelines), clearly marked with the child's name, and ensure the child knows where it is.
● Encourage older children to take responsibility for their inhaler.
● Make sure that a child's reliever inhaler is always at hand and encourage the child to use it as soon as an attack begins. Parents/carers may also advise you to use it *before* physical activity or other events that might trigger an attack.
● Stay calm and reassure the child. Reliever inhalers usually work quickly to relax the muscles. Do not put your arm around the shoulders as this can restrict breathing.
● Help the child to breathe slowly and deeply by breathing with them.
● When the attack is over, help the child return to normal activities.
● If the medication does not work after five to ten minutes, if the child is too distressed to talk or if you are worried about their condition, call an ambulance. Parents/carers can tell you what would constitute an emergency in their child's case.
● Make sure colleagues and mid-day supervisory assistants know what to look out for and what they should do.

Finding out more
The National Asthma Campaign publishes various documents: write to Providence House, Providence Place, London N1 0NT (tel: 0207 226 2260), or visit www.asthma.org.uk.

WORKING WITH CARERS
● When the child joins the school, talk to parents or carers about what seem to be the triggers for their child's asthma and what steps you should take. Bring this information up to date whenever the child moves up a class.

MAKING LINKS
● Contact your local health visitor for general advice on coping with asthma. Various videos and advice leaflets are available from most NHS Trusts.
See also the page on Allergy (page 10) since eczema is a form of allergic reaction.

Attention difficulties and AD/HD

What you need to know
● Some children have attention difficulties that are greater than for other children their age. This is because they have a physiological difference in their brains controlling their arousal system.
● They might have been diagnosed with 'attention deficit disorder' with or without 'hyperactivity'. This is known collectively as *attention deficit/hyperactivity disorder* or 'AD/HD'. It can be helped through careful behaviour management and also sometimes through medication (such as Ritalin® or Concerta®).
● Usually, medication is not prescribed until children are old enough to say how the medicine makes them feel – usually about age six – because side effects can be unpleasant and suppress appetite.
● You might find yourself working with parents/carers, doctors or psychologists to assess whether a pupil has AD/HD, perhaps by completing a questionnaire or by observation. This is because that diagnosis is only made if the child displays the difficulty in more than one situation, usually home and school. However, you do not need a diagnosis in order to support the child. It makes more sense for you to identify that a child has difficulties in attention and concentration and plan the best approaches to help.

How to help
● Children with short attention spans benefit from clear routines and structures so that they know what is going to happen and when. Sandwich short periods of sustained concentration and effort with periods of time when the child can be more active or have a free choice in his or her learning.
● Give strong encouragement and praise to keep learning enjoyable, attention-getting and motivating.
● Break tasks down into simpler steps so that a child with a short attention span can still learn from them.
● Find a distraction-free space to work in for activities that require sustained concentration, looking or listening and work in smaller groups. For example, set up an 'office space' on a side table.
● Make sure you have eye contact before speaking to the child and use his or her name and perhaps a touch to gain attention. Be prepared to give reminders constantly.
● Give clear, short directions, showing and telling the child what to do.
● Use positive behaviour management to build up to desired behaviours step by small step.
● Keep careful observations in order to help doctors and parents/carers monitor any changes in medication or behaviour.

Finding out more
Attention Deficit/Hyperactivity Disorder – A Practical guide for Teachers by Paul Cooper and Katherine Ideus (David Fulton).

WORKING WITH CARERS
● Share what approaches seem to work best with parents and carers. Offer them advice on dealing with difficult behaviour and provide support during what is probably a trying time for them.
● Try to establish a role for the school in helping to monitor any medication so that the child is on the lowest dose necessary to improve their learning.

MAKING LINKS
● Most NHS Trusts have a service for identifying and supporting children with AD/HD. The health visitor, school doctor or educational psychologist is likely to know more about this.
● See also the page on Behaviour difficulties (page 15) for information on a behaviour management approach.

Autistic spectrum difficulties

What you need to know
● Some children appear indifferent to other people and behave as if they are 'in a world of their own'. They might have been diagnosed as having 'autism', 'autistic features' or 'Asperger's Syndrome' (page 11). All these conditions have some overlap and are described as forming 'the autistic spectrum' of difficulties.

- The children may not learn co-operatively with others and only join in activities if an adult insists and assists.
- Children with 'autism' may have very little language, they might echo what is said to them, or they might talk in a very stereotyped way.
- Sometimes, they might become absorbed in arranging toys, collecting certain objects, or spinning or turning objects repeatedly to watch them move.
- Eye contact might be very poor and they might not be able to play imaginatively, unless in a very stereotyped way.
- Behaviour might be bizarre or very fearful, especially if familiar routines are disturbed or if they feel stressed.

How to help
● Start by helping the child feel settled when working one-to-one with a key worker. Gradually involve one or more other children at the table but stay close by to support and assist.
● Play games that involve taking turns, for example throwing a dice for each other to count. The idea here is that the child will begin to see your company as useful and fun.
● Try to keep to a familiar and structured routine. Take a series of photographs of the typical school day and show the child these to illustrate what is happening next.
● Provide a simple commentary to the child about what he or she is doing; 'Jack is *writing*'. This helps the child link language to action.
● Provide plenty of encouragement whenever the child communicates with you, whether by voice, eye contact or through actions.
● Support the child's choice of activities, but distract the child if he or she becomes too absorbed or obsessed with them.
● Where you have free activity, work or play alongside the child imitating them so that they begin to see that their actions influence what you do. Move on to sharing a plaything or activity together.
● Provide a quiet 'safe base' where the child can go to if they feel overloaded. Provide favourite music or an activity there for relaxing.
● Demonstrate to the other children ways of involving the child.

Finding out more
The National Autistic Society provides advice for carers and professionals. Contact them at 393 City Road, London EC1V 1NG, 0870 600 85 85, www.nas.org.uk.

WORKING WITH CARERS
● Photographs of daily routines can be used at home as well to help autistic children understand what is happening when.

MAKING LINKS
● You are likely to need advice from your LEA Support Service. There might also be a Specialist Autism Team who can provide information, advice and training.
● See also the pages on Asperger's Syndrome (page 11) and Semantic Pragmatic Difficulties (page 51), since the conditions overlap, and Behaviour difficulties (opposite) for a behavioural management approach.

Behaviour difficulties

What you need to know
● If a child has had time to settle with you and is not responding to your usual encouragement and boundary setting, despite all your usual approaches, then you might consider talking to parents/carers about additional or different approaches.
● These are the children who you would describe as having 'behaviour difficulties' and who would benefit from being on your SEN register and having a within-school individual behaviour plan. There are four main criteria for helping you to decide that a behaviour is abnormal or problematic:

'**fixation**': A behaviour has continued beyond the age where it might be considered appropriate. For example, a child of seven is still throwing huge temper tantrums.
'**regression**': A behaviour might have been achieved successfully at an appropriate age and the child then reverts back to behaviour characteristic of a younger age. For example, a child suddenly becomes very tearful on arrival at school.
'**failure to display**': A behaviour that should have developed by a particular age has not done so. For examples, a child of nine does not have the skills to make and keep a friend.
'**exaggeration**': A normal behaviour such as a burst of frustration might become exaggerated into a full-blown temper tantrum in which other children might get hurt.

How to help
● Always talk in terms of 'problem behaviour' rather than 'problem children' since most potential for change lies in how everyone else *manages* that behaviour.
● Start by standing back and observing a child's behaviour. Work out what behaviour you wish to change, what led up to the difficult behaviour and what the consequences were. This is an 'ABC' observation (antecedent, behaviour, consequence). From this, work out how you can change the A, the B, or the C.
● You might be able to avoid certain situations altogether for a while (like assembly), encourage another more appropriate behaviour (taking turns in an activity instead of dominating it), distract the child with something else to do (using playground games) or teach a new social skill (such as holding a conversation).
● Use praise and rewards when the child is behaving appropriately. Make sure that any sanctions you use are not rewarding – for example, sitting in the staffroom where the biscuits are!

Finding out more
Activities for including children with behavioural difficulties by Hannah Mortimer, from this series.

WORKING WITH CARERS
● Always discuss behaviour difficulties with parents and carers but make it clear *why* you are doing this – in order to solve a problem together rather than to blame them. Find a way to word your concerns constructively, using 'and' rather than 'but' statements where possible. For example 'He's so enthusiastic at school *and* I would like to help him make more friends. At the moment, the others are wary of him'.

MAKING LINKS
● Talk with your SENCO for ideas on behaviour management and see page 36 to help you write your individual behaviour/education plan.
● See also 'Aggression' (page 9), which is one common form of behaviour difficulty.

Bereavement

What you need to know
● Each day, 40 000 families worldwide experience the death of a child. Many will face the death of a relative at some time, and children may come across death early in their lives.
● Younger children find it hard to accept the permanence of death.
● Most of us, children included, move through stages of denial, grief, anger, guilt and readjustment. All these feelings are normal, take time and are best supported by those nearest and dearest to us.
● Grieving only needs outside support if it becomes 'stuck'.

How to help
● When someone in one of the families attending your school dies, try not to let your embarrassment and fear of not knowing what to say get in the way of speaking to the family.
● Avoid giving direct advice and platitudes – 'time will heal' or 'you're taking it so well' – but be sensitive to what practical help you can give. Perhaps you can provide additional support to any siblings or friends in school who are grieving in their own individual ways.
● Be there to listen. If one of the children has died, find happy memories to share, and continue to talk about the child.
● Do give extra attention to siblings or friends who will be feeling confused and sad just when the adults around them may not have the time or emotional resources to comfort them.
● Talk about what has happened in clear, absolute terms. Work and play alongside the child and provide opportunities for them to act out some of their feelings.
● Other children too will want to talk about things. Do not be put off if the children seem almost callous in their response. The news is usually taken at a very practical level with concerns like 'who will his mum collect from school now?' or 'who will get his bike now?'
● Try to avoid using expressions that will confuse children. If you talk of death being 'like going to sleep for ever', you can leave them frightened about what will happen if they fall asleep at night.
● When the child is ready to join in fully again, set work that is slightly easier than usual so that they can succeed despite their difficulties in concentration.

Finding out more
The Child Bereavement Trust can be contacted at Aston House, West Wycombe, High Wycombe, Buckinghamshire. HP14 3AG, www.childbereavement.org.uk. Barnardo's 'Memory Store' and 'Memory Book' are designed for children facing separation, loss and bereavement: Barnardo's Child Care Publications, Barnardo's Trading Estate, Paycocke Road, Basildon, Essex, SS14 3DR, www.barnardos.org.uk.

WORKING WITH CARERS
● Do encourage the family to take things steadily and not try to do too much at once. They may need continual reassurance that decisions they have taken were right and the best for their child.
● Siblings may need reassurance too so that they do not feel they caused, or could have prevented, the death in some way.

MAKING LINKS
● Most hospital paediatric departments have a specialist nurse who helps with bereavement counselling and advice.
● See also 'Cancer and leukaemia' (opposite) if a child with this condition is terminally ill.

Cancer and leukaemia

What you need to know
● In a cancer, certain cells multiply too quickly and sometimes a tumour is formed, perhaps in the brain or the bowel.
● It is usually adults who are affected but some cancers do affect children and the most common is leukaemia.
● Leukaemia is a rare form of cancer affecting the white blood cells. Children become anaemic, their blood does not clot properly and they cannot fight infections well. So the first symptoms are increased bruising, infection and tiredness. You might also see recurrent nose bleeds, a purplish rash and the child might complain that joints are painful.
● The outlook for children with leukaemia is so much better than it used to be, with at least half being completely cured. However, the child might need considerable time in hospital or lengthy treatment.

● Treatments vary greatly depending on the patient and the cancer. The most common involve strong drugs or radiotherapy. Modern medical practice is much better at controlling unpleasant side effects.
● Unfortunately these medicines also attack the hair cells and that is why the children sometimes lose their hair for a while.
● These children are likely to need hospital check-ups for several years in case there is a return of the cancer.
● Children receiving or recovering from treatment will be more prone than usual to infections.

How to help
● If you are worried about a child's symptoms, have a quiet word with parents/carers or a school nurse so that these can be medically checked, without alarming them with your reasons.
● Look for ways of keeping your links with a child who is in hospital. Encourage the children in the class to send letters, cards and photographs, building this into your literacy work.
● Keep close contact with the family so that you can send distracting activities and non-stressful work once the child has more energy and is ready to 'get back into gear'.
● Make up a story or give some science background in order to prepare the rest of the class for welcoming back a child after treatment. If you know that the child looks different in some way (perhaps because of hair loss), explain to the other children how strong medicines were needed to fight the illness but that these also damaged the hair cells for a while. Explain that hair can grow again.

Finding out more
Sargent Cancer Care for Children is based at Griffin House, 161 Hammersmith Road, London W6 8SG, www.sargent.org.

WORKING WITH CARERS
● If a cancer or leukaemia has been diagnosed, keep closely in touch with the family and help to keep up the morale of family, siblings and friends while the child is away.
● When a child is being treated or is still convalescing, warn parents/carers if there are any infectious diseases in the school such as chicken pox.

MAKING LINKS
● Ask parents/carers for the name of the child's specialist cancer nurse so that you can ask how you can best support the child and family over this time.
● You may be able to work closely with the cancer nurse and also any hospice involved.
● See 'Medical difficulties' (page 36) and 'Bereavement' (page 16).

SPECIAL NEEDS in the primary years

Cerebral palsy

What you need to know

● About 1500 babies are born with or develop cerebral palsy every year in Britain. It is caused when part of the foetus' brain is not working properly so that body movements cannot be coordinated.

● Sometimes the brain injury is caused by an early infection during pregnancy or sometimes from a bleed in the brain in very premature babies. Another possible cause is a loss of oxygen to the brain, or sometimes the brain has not developed normally for some other reason. The effect of this is that the messages from brain to muscles and back again become jumbled.

● Though cerebral palsy cannot be cured, the condition that can be worked on with therapy and encouragement so that the child is affected as little as possible.

● Symptoms might be very slight, or so severe that the child needs help in every day-to-day task. Movements may be slow and awkward, floppy or stiff, poorly controlled or unwanted. Some children will be in wheelchairs or use walking frames. Others might have an unsteady gait or find it difficult to balance.

● You must never assume that, because children have considerable physical difficulties, they will also be slow in their thinking and intelligence.

How to help

● Clearly, these children will not have had the same early learning experiences as children without a physical difficulty, so here is where your school can help to redress the balance. Make sure that the curriculum you provide is fully accessible to the child by making reasonable adjustments; both in your physical spaces and in the lessons you plan. Think about each learning activity and how you can involve the child who has physical difficulties.

● Perhaps an activity can be rearranged at floor level. Perhaps all the children in that class can sit on chairs during assembly so that they are at the same height as the wheelchair.

● Keep floor spaces clear from obstacles and child-friendly for any pupils using walking frames or wheelchairs.

● From late 2004, all your school buildings and facilities should be accessible to people with disabilities.

Finding out more

SCOPE, 6 Market Road, London N7 9PW runs a cerebral palsy helpline, free on 0800 800 3333, or visit www.scope.org.uk.

WORKING WITH CARERS

● Seating, posture and positioning are vitally important to prevent later problems in bones. Talk to parents/carers about the correct approaches.

● Some children with cerebral palsy use highly sophisticated equipment to aid their communication. If possible, ask the child to teach you about it, and find out from parents/carers or therapists how to 'troubleshoot' if it goes wrong.

MAKING LINKS

● Therapists will also be able to help you involve the child in PE in a way that makes the best use of their movements. Find out what you need to do to manage toilet routines, mealtimes, and dressing in order to encourage independence.

● See also 'Physical difficulties' (page 45) and 'Disability Act' (page 25), which will help you ensure equal opportunities for children who are affected.

Child Protection

What you need to know
- Everyone who comes into contact with children on a regular basis has a duty to safeguard and promote their welfare.
- Each school should have a copy of the local procedures set jointly by the LEA, health service and social services departments. These are statutory and must be adhered to.
- Each school should have arranged staff training in child protection.
- It is up to each individual to make sure they are aware of the child protection procedures in that school and LEA.
- Social services involvement has increased since the Children Act 1989 and you might have to work with a social worker, providing information about a child during a child protection enquiry or taking part in a multi agency assessment.
- Social services can also provide you with general advice.
- If you are concerned that a child is being abused, you must refer these concerns to social services or police, usually through the head/SENCO or the designated contact for child protection.
- Child abuse can take different forms: physical (as in marks, bruises and injuries), sexual (and the child may have disclosed some information to you), emotional or neglect (perhaps the child is noticeably failing to thrive).
- Initial concerns might be what the child has said, unexplained bruises or marks which you notice during PE, inappropriate sexualised behaviour, or sexually or violently graphic artwork.

How to help
- Always keep records of incidents, what was said, what you did.
- Always be ready to listen to the child. Repeat back what the child has said to check you have understood correctly.
- Do not promise confidentiality – you cannot keep information confidential if a child is at risk or if there are criminal implications. Instead, explain that you have a duty to make sure that the child is safe though you will not do anything without first telling the child and explaining what will happen next.
- Do not use leading questions, which might later distort evidence.
- Make sure you are not putting yourself in a vulnerable position which might lead to allegations against your own behaviour.
- The protection of the child is absolutely paramount. If you are not sure whether you should be taking action, contact your school's education social worker for advice.
- If you make a telephone referral, confirm it in writing within 48 hours.

Finding out more
Send for the booklet: *What To Do If You're Worried a Child is Being Abused* (ref. 31815) from the Department of Health Publications. 0207 210 4850, www.publications.doh.gov.uk/safeguardingchildren.

WORKING WITH CARERS
- If you make a referral to social services and/or Police, agree with that agency what the child and parents/carers will be told, by whom and when.

MAKING LINKS
- Your local social services department will provide you with advice or take action if you are concerned – contact the local duty officer.

Code of Practice for SEN

What you need to know

● The *Code of Practice for SEN* was published by the DfES was revised in 2002 and all schools in England must have regard to its guidance. There are similar documents for Wales, Scotland and Northern Ireland.

● It provides information on how to identify, assess, intervene and monitor children with special educational needs in your school. Instead of the five-stage approach of the 'old' Code of Practice, there is a graded approach to identifying and meeting SEN. This is in three phases: School Action (where the school assesses and meets the SEN, page 47), School Action Plus (where the school brings on board outside professional help, page 48) and Statemented provision (where the LEA determines and monitors the SEN, page 60).

● Individual Education Plans (IEPs) should be a key feature of planning for any SEN in your class (see page 36). The SENCO will help you to design and monitor these and will explain your duties to review these regularly. The SENCO should also provide you with general information, basic training and advice needed to meet your duties. You are not expected to be an 'expert' straight away.

● There is a move towards greater inclusion for all children, further strengthened by the SEN Disability Act (page 25).

How to help

● Ask your SENCO to give basic training in the Code so that you are aware of what it means for your school.

● If you feel that a child may have special needs, the SENCO should help you assess the child's difficulties, plan interventions and work with parents and carers to ensure the child makes

reasonable progress in spite of their needs.

● It is each teacher's responsibility to identify and meet special educational needs – not just the SENCO's – but you will need the support and advice of the SENCO or other professionals to do this. Contact the LEA Support Service, Educational Psychology Service or Advisory Team for information on SEN training.

Finding out more

Copies of the Code can be obtained from DfES Publications at: PO Box 5050, Sherwood Park, Annesley, Nottinghamshire NG15 0DJ, quoting reference DfES 581/2001. *Removing Barriers to Achievement: the Government's Strategy for SEN* is available from the DfES and can be accessed at www.teachernet.gov.uk/wholeschool/sen/senstrategy.

WORKING WITH CARERS

● There should be a greater involvement with parents and carers, who now have more rights and wider choices.

● Parents and carers should always be informed and involved when you are planning for their child's SEN using the framework provided in the SEN Code of Practice.

MAKING LINKS

● You may find yourself working with members of the LEA Pupil and Parents Support team for your area, perhaps alongside a support teacher, education social worker, advisory teacher or psychologist. They can provide advice on your IEP, approaches and monitoring.
See also the entry on Individual education plans (page 36).

Cystic fibrosis

What you need to know

- Some children are born with this condition, which affects about one in 2000 children.
- For these children, the mucous glands produce abnormally thick, sticky mucus and their sweat glands produce excess salt. Though their lungs will have been normal at birth, each time they have an infection this sticky mucus collects in the lungs and blocks airways causing further damage.
- Most children with CF will be able to participate fully in classroom activities though they might need a modified curriculum for PE.
- Their pancreas will be affected too. The small channels which normally allow enzymes to flow into the intestine become blocked leading to cysts. That is why these children often need to take oral digestive enzymes at mealtimes.
- Children with cystic fibrosis have daily physiotherapy to help drain the mucus from various parts of the lungs.

How to help

- Make sure the child leads as normal a life as possible. Apart from having physiotherapy, taking enzymes and doing specific exercises every day, the child should be able to do what most other children their age can do. Your task is to make them feel like everyone else.
- Accept the child's need to cough in class and to get rid of mucus. On hot days, you may need to remind the child to take extra salt. Parents/carers will let you know what to do and when.
- The child will probably need to take regular enzymes at each mealtime. If these are missed, the child will begin to feel tired, get tummy ache, and need to go to the toilet a lot.
- Expect the child to be absent from time to time for medical check-ups or when they are fighting infections.
- Plan approaches for helping the child to keep up to date with any missed lessons, for example by providing notes and summaries and sending work home where appropriate. If absences are frequent, it is best to do this *anyway* rather than wait until the child has been away for over a week or so.
- Have a quiet area that the child can settle into if they are feeling particularly tired, but encourage physical exercise. Parents/carers will tell you how much exercise their child should be getting each day. Exercise helps the lungs to stay fitter.
- Keep parents/carers informed of any infections going around. Though most children with CF are encouraged to keep attending, additional antibiotics might be needed.

Finding out more

The Cystic Fibrosis Trust can be contacted at: 11 London Road, Bromley BR1 1BY (tel: 0208 464 7211), www.cftrust.org.uk.

WORKING WITH CARERS
- Talk with parents/carers to make sure that you have everything you need to know about their child's condition. Children may be affected differently so this information is important to have.

MAKING LINKS
- Ask parents/carers to introduce you to their physiotherapist so that you can make sure you are doing all you should be to support the child.
- Sometimes the physiotherapy can be arranged within school. Try to provide a quiet area and also to keep this inclusive by allowing the child to have their friends around them if they would like to and it is break-time.
- See also the entry on Medical difficulties (page 40).

DCD/Dyspraxia

What you need to know

● Children whose development of motor co-ordination is impaired may be described as having 'developmental co-ordination disorder' or 'dyspraxia'. The diagnosis is usually only made if the impairment significantly interferes with educational progress or daily activities.

● These children appear clumsy. They find it hard to move and balance smoothly. They may be poor in organising themselves, find it hard to speak clearly and difficult to understand where their body is in space, so that they knock into things.

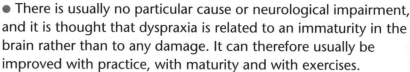

● Compared to other children their age, these children may find it hard to dress and undress quickly for PE, have a poor pen grip, find design and technology difficult, and be poorly balanced when running or climbing.

● They may hide the extent of their difficulties by trying to avoid certain situations such as PE or avoiding writing.

● There is usually no particular cause or neurological impairment, and it is thought that dyspraxia is related to an immaturity in the brain rather than to any damage. It can therefore usually be improved with practice, with maturity and with exercises.

● By Key Stage 2 the child may still present as rather clumsy, with poor organisation skills and untidy writing. Poor co-ordination and social skills may also be apparent.

How to help

● Keep physical activities as fun and motivating as possible. Children with dyspraxia need lots of practice but will soon 'opt out' if the activities are repetitive and beyond their ability.

● If a child is verbally dyspraxic (and therefore does not speak clearly), repeat back unclear language clearly in order to check that you have understood and to provide a model for them to listen to.

● Take time to talk the child through visual information such as graphs, diagrams, flowcharts, plans and maps, as dyspraxic difficulties often cause visual perceptual problems as well.

● Start fine-motor tasks with larger materials (such as model making in D&T) and progress to smaller materials as skills develop.

● Look for motivating ways of encouraging 'clever fingers', such as piano/keyboard and computer activities.

● Make sure that the chair is the right height for the child's feet to be firmly on the floor when sitting at a table.

Finding out more

The Dyspraxia Foundation is at: 8 West Alley, Hitchin, SG5 1EG. 01462 454986, www.dyspraxiafoundation.org.uk.

WORKING WITH CARERS

● Provide ideas for developing independence skills such as dressing, undressing and personal organisation at home.

● Send home activities for encouraging writing skills using game-like approaches that will be motivating to the child and family.

MAKING LINKS

● Many children with dyspraxia are helped by occupational therapists who provide exercises to improve co-ordination. If a child is having difficulty in scanning written text fluently, suggest an assessment by an orthoptist who is specialised in 'visual dyslexia'. Your local optician or eye hospital should have information on this. See also the entry on Specific learning difficulties (page 56).

Developmental delay

What you need to know

● All children vary widely in the age at which they reach various developmental stages such as lacing their shoes, knowing their letters and numbers or balancing on one leg. It is quite normal to have a wide variation in your class.

● However, some children fail to achieve their developmental milestones within the usual time range and are sometimes described as being 'delayed' in their development.

● In older children, developmental delay manifests itself in the child attaining National Curriculum levels normally but at a slower pace than most of the other children in the class.

● For some children, there might be a clear cause – perhaps they have a chromosomal condition such as Down's syndrome (page 26) or perhaps they have not yet had the necessary experiences and opportunities in which to learn and to develop.

● For others, there may be no known cause; it is simply that a child seems to be taking longer than other children to progress.

● Some children will catch up eventually, others may continue to have difficulties. The help that you should provide is the same.

How to help

● Use a phased intervention following the guidance of the SEN Code of Practice (page 20). The level of support does not depend on the label (for example whether the child has Down's syndrome) but on how the child progresses and the additional or different approaches that you need to put into place to help them learn.

● Keep story times and discussion times simple and use props for the child to look at and handle.

● Emphasise key words and keep language simple. Establish eye contact before speaking to engage the child's attention fully.

● Encourage the development of all three learning styles (visual, auditory and kinaesthetic) by using multi-sensory approaches which involve seeing, listening and doing.

● Keep activities short, and end on a successful note.

● Use praise and encouragement to make the child feel successful.

● Look for opportunities in which the child *needs* to communicate, by offering choices and encouraging initiative. Try to avoid the *learned helplessness* that can develop if things are provided 'on a plate'.

● Use a structured step-by-step approach for teaching new skills.

● Use small groups to encourage language and listening.

● Provide materials so the child can participate fully (triangular pen holds for immature writing, squeezy scissors, counting aids and number lines to assist basic maths, easier tasks and activities).

Finding out more

Visit www.mencap.org.uk for advice on learning disabilities. There is a regular web newsletter and links to other useful sites.

WORKING WITH CARERS
● Keep regular contact with parents and carers so that you can be kept in touch with any therapy goals from other professionals.

MAKING LINKS
● Contact your SENCO for information about LEA learning support services in your area. See also 'Learning difficulties' (page 39).

Diabetes

What you need to know

● Diabetes is caused when there is not enough insulin produced in the body. Insulin is a hormone produced in the pancreas. It is responsible for glucose metabolism and it helps us to store glucose ready for when energy is needed.

● There are about 15 to 20 children per 100 000 diagnosed with diabetes each year and this is increasing.

● There are two forms of diabetes; one affecting children and young adults and one starting in middle age. Most children have Type 1 or 'insulin dependent diabetes mellitus' in which the insulin-producing cells of the pancreas have been destroyed.

● It can start quite suddenly at any age, and it can run in families.

● The first symptoms you might notice are excessive thirst, large amounts of urine being passed frequently, weight loss, irritability and tiredness, an unusual smell of pear drops to the breath and a reduced resistance to infections.

● It is diagnosed through a blood test and children are usually prescribed regular insulin to control their blood sugar.

● Many older children give insulin injections to themselves and can also learn how to test their blood and urine sugar levels.

● If the child's blood sugar level falls too low, this is called a hypoglycaemic episode or a 'hypo'.

How to help

● Many children who have diabetes have the condition under control and it should not affect your time together in school, apart from the need to look out for a sugar 'hypo'.

● Hypo symptoms include hunger, sweating, drowsiness, pallor, glazed eyes, shaking, poor concentration and irritability.

● These symptoms can be treated using sugary drinks/chocolate, as agreed with medical staff and parents or carers.

● Most parents/carers will send in snacks that might be necessary before the child does physical exercise. They might ask you to have a sugary drink on hand for their child at these times.

● Make sure the child never misses a meal or snack time.

● If parents/carers need you to check sugar levels and this has been agreed with the school, let them show you how to use equipment.

● Let parents/carers know when there are infections in your school; sometimes this means different insulin requirements.

● Make sure that catering staff know any implications. Even if a child brings packed lunches, there will be occasions such as celebrations when snack choices suitable for diabetic children might be needed.

Finding out more

Diabetes UK is based at: 10 Queen Anne Street, London W1M 0BD (www.diabetes.org.uk), or contact the Juvenile Diabetes Research Foundation, 25 Gosfield Street, London, W1W 6EB (www.jdrf.org.uk).

WORKING WITH CARERS

● Talk to parents or carers about their child's regime. What special diet and medication is the child on? What signs will you see when the child's blood sugar has fallen too low and what should you do about it?

MAKING LINKS

● The local health visitors will be able to give you more information and advice if you need it. Make sure that you have the name and address of the child's GP in case information is needed quickly. Hypos are not usually very dangerous, but if you are concerned, telephone Accident and Emergency for advice.

● See also the entry on Medical Difficulties (page 40).

Disability Act

What you need to know

● The Disability Discrimination Act (DDA) 1995 brought in legal measures to clarify disabled people's rights in terms of employment and obtaining goods, services, transport, land or property.
● The Act was amended to cover the requirements on establishments which provide education for children and this formed the Special Educational Need and Disability Act (SENDA) 2001.
● Under the Act, a disabled person has 'a physical or mental impairment, which has an effect on his or her ability to carry out normal day to day activities. That effect must be substantial (not trivial or minor), adverse and long-term'.
● Schools are required to overcome physical features that impede access to a service. They will have to make 'reasonable adjustments' to the environment to overcome physical barriers to access both for pupils and for disabled adults.

How to help

● You cannot refuse a service (such as education), offer a worse standard of service or offer a service on worse terms to a disabled child or person unless you can offer a 'justification'. This is called the 'less favourable treatment' duty. Even so, you will be expected to demonstrate that you are planning ahead to improve access and inclusion in the future.

● You need to plan 'reasonable adjustments' for disabled children. This might include training for personal support assistants, planning accessible activities in an accessible environment, flexibility in terms of toilet arrangements and the provision of flexible transport.
● Plan school outings well ahead so that children with disabilities can be included.
● If you are short of staff on an outing, it would probably be seen as a 'reasonable adjustment' to invite a parent or carer to come too in order to help.
● Make sure that children who cannot walk or stand are not left out – plan an alternative activity which is at floor level.
● Plan ways of including all the children in group and circle time. If a child is non-verbal, look for alternative ways they can join in, answer the register, and so on.
● Teach staff members some basic sign language and share this with all the children.
● Always keep records that explain why you are making adjustments and how you are monitoring their effectiveness.

Finding out more

Get copies of 'Highlights' information sheets 186 and 187 from the National Children's Bureau, 8 Wakley Street, London, EC1V 7QE (www.ncb.org.uk).

WORKING WITH CARERS
● Make sure that your admissions policy states that your school does not discriminate against disabled pupils in any of the services it provides.

MAKING LINKS
● Joint meetings with outside professionals and with parents and carers would also be seen as useful steps towards planning your 'reasonable adjustments'.
See also the information on Inclusion (page 37).

Down's syndrome

What you need to know

● The word 'syndrome' means a collection of signs and characteristics. Most people with Down's syndrome have certain facial and other physical characteristics that make them appear similar. However, it is important to realise that there are far more differences between people with Down's syndrome than similarities. Each child is an individual in his or her own right and we need to recognise and respect this.

● One baby in about 1000 is born with Down's syndrome. It is caused by an additional chromosome in each body cell. People with Down's syndrome have 47 chromosomes instead of the usual 46. This results in the development of the growing baby in the womb becoming disrupted and altered.

● The chances of a baby being born with Down's syndrome increases with the mother's age, particularly over the age of 35. This is one of the reasons older mothers are screened during pregnancy.

● Many children with Down's syndrome are healthy but 40% have heart problems at birth and some might need surgery. There is also a much higher risk of hearing difficulties, vision needs careful monitoring and there is a tendency towards more frequent infections and chestiness too.

● Children with Down's syndrome usually have a greater difficulty learning than the majority of children their age.

How to help

● Get to know the child as an individual. Find out about his or her likes, dislikes, strengths and weaknesses using your usual methods of observation and assessment.

● Look carefully at your curriculum and in particular the literacy and numeracy frameworks. You will find it helpful to break your learning goals down into finer steps so that you can obtain a 'baseline' or starting point for teaching.

● If necessary, track back to the Foundation Stage curriculum with its Early Learning Goals and Stepping Stones if you need to start from an earlier level.

● You may also find the P Scales helpful if a child has severe learning difficulties. These are developmentally early goals which can be used for effective target setting for pupils with SEN. Send for the DfES document *Supporting the Target Setting Process* (DfES 0065/2001).

● Plan learning opportunities that help the child to generalise what has been learned from one situation to another.

Finding out more

The Down's Syndrome Association is based at: Langdon Down Centre, 2a Langdon Park, Teddington TW11 9PS, 0208 682 4001 www.downs-syndrome.org.uk.

WORKING WITH CARERS

● Keep closely in touch with parents/ carers so that you can celebrate achievements at home and in school and build on them.

● Meet regularly to plan progress, step by small step.

● Notify parents/ carers if there are nasty infections in the class so that they can take extra precautions if necessary.

MAKING LINKS

● The child might be known to the local Child Development Centre who would be able to provide further advice and information. Otherwise, involve your local pupil support services in the usual way.

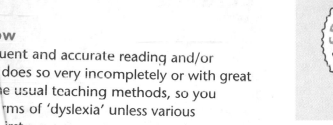

D

...ow

...luent and accurate reading and/or
...does so very incompletely or with great
...he usual teaching methods, so you
...rms of 'dyslexia' unless various
...irst.

...ecific learning difficulty' since the level
...are much lower than one might
...ual ability or general oral ability.
...dyslexia are boys. The condition
...his is not always the case.
...he or several of: poor sequencing
...tion and memory, poor visual
...r poor short-term memory.
...learning difficulties so that
...ed in exams.

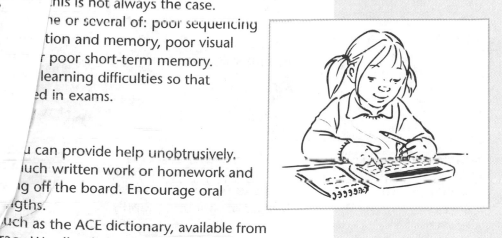

...u can provide help unobtrusively.
...uch written work or homework and
...g off the board. Encourage oral
...gths.
...uch as the ACE dictionary, available from
...racy Wordbank, available from John Lewis
...0.co.uk).
...es of ICT, such as editing tools and spell checks.
...ifferent forms of presenting their work, such as
...el-point notes or even by recording their voice.
...ks into smaller steps and help the child organise
...begun.
...hat the child reads out loud.
...sory teaching approaches that allow you to use
...pport weaknesses.
...arged photocopies of worksheets that carry a lot of
...this makes them easier to use.
● a lot of copying to be done, provide a photocopy of the
...p instead. Encourage highlighting to mark important points.
● Avoid a sense of failure so that the child is not frustrated.
...ge the child to present their creativity in other ways.
● Ta... the SENCO if small group or individual tuition is necessary.
...h study skills and mind mapping.

...ding out more

...e British Dyslexia Association is at 98 London Road, Reading, RG1
...(www.bda-dyslexia.org.uk). Contact The Dyslexia Institute at
...k House, Wick Road, Egham, Surrey, TW20 0HH
...w.dyslexia-inst.org.uk) for details of assessment/tuition centres.

WORKING WITH CARERS
● Ask parents or carers to have an up to date eye check if visual scanning is a problem, preferably with an orthoptist.

MAKING LINKS
● If a child is receiving private dyslexia tuition, try to make contact with the tutor so that you can work together.
You will find a mention of dyscalculia on the page covering specific learning difficulties (page 56).

Eczema

What you need to know
● Some children have a very itchy, dry, scaly, red rash on their neck, their hands and in the creases of their limbs. children, this is widespread and can be debilitating. For are just sore or irritating patches. This is 'eczema' and is common allergic reaction. It tends to run in families wh hay fever and asthma.
● Some children have the condition so severely that the constant discomfort. It can come and go in severity with and bad spells, sometimes related to the time of year.
● The most common form (atopic eczema) typically dev first few months and most children do grow out of it by they are around three. By the time they start school, mos eczema will have improved.
● Eczema can be triggered by certain foods (such as dairy eggs or wheat). An attack can also be set off by stress. It m caused by skin irritants such as wool, washing detergents

How to help
● Find out about any special diet. You may need to ask par carers to send in a special snack for their child or some soy instead of your usual supply.
● Ask if there is anything that their child cannot handle. Fo example, some find working with clay difficult as it can dry Others need to wash hands after handling certain craft mate
● Washing hands a lot can dry them out, so help the child to or her hands thoroughly and ask parents/carers about a mois cream if this will help.
● Do not let your concern show itself as anxiety. If a child is i and upset by their condition, they need you to stay calm and distract them as far as possible.
● Children who have severe eczema can be exhausted in scho because of disturbed nights. Sometimes, you may have to pro somewhere for a tired child to rest.
● Use distraction to discourage scratching and rubbing.
● Be flexible about any school uniform so that the child can be comfortable and any affected limbs are covered. A loose cotton tracksuit is usually best for PE.
● Pay attention to room temperature – heat or cold can be uncomfortable for a child with severe eczema. If a child is uncomfortable during PE, make sure there is an open window that any child can use to have a cool down.

Finding out more
Ask your local health visitor or GP for pamphlets about the conditi or visit the National Eczema Organisation's website, www.eczema.

WORKING WITH CARERS
● Find out from parents/carers whether there are known triggers for their child's eczema. It may be that you need to avoid physical contact with pets, or make sure they do not handle certain materials.
● Encourage parents and carers to keep the child's nails short and clean to reduce scratching and infection.

MAKING LINKS
● If you have a child with very severe eczema due to attend your class, consider asking their health visitor or school nurse to advise you on their care and any particular precautions you need to take.

Emotional difficulties

What you need to know

● Emotional difficulties in children can take many forms and can stem from many sources. It is most important to address these early in order to prevent mental health problems developing in adulthood.

● Sometimes children seem extremely shy and continue to cry or to be withdrawn long after you feel they should have settled with you.

● Others cannot seem to cope with newness, with failure or with correction. They might destroy their own work or creations as if they did not matter and behave as if they were not bothered by your praise and encouragement.

● Some older children may attempt to harm themselves, to bully others or to abuse substances.

How to help

● Think about the child's self-esteem (page 50) and about ways in which you can encourage and support him or her. Perhaps the child is feeling under pressure in some way. Can you think of anything that would help this? Can you perhaps expect a little less of them for a while, and boost their confidence as much as possible?

● If the child suddenly becomes very anxious and quiet, or behaves in a completely different way (and seems unable to tell you why), then you should talk with parents/carers to try to get to the bottom of it. Remember the child protection procedures (page 19).

● Having predictable routines, clear boundaries for behaviour and familiar people in their lives generally makes children feel more secure.

● Use circle time approaches to help all the children develop self-confidence, a positive self-image and good looking and listening skills.

● If you suspect bullying is going on, consider adopting a problem-solving approach that addresses the issue but also teaches the children to become more sensitive in their dealings with each other. *Crying for help: The no blame approach to bullying* by George Robinson and Barbara Maines (Lucky Duck Publishing) provides useful suggestions.

● Make sure you cover issues such as appropriate assertiveness, bullying and substance abuse as part of your personal and social education curriculum.

Finding out more

The publication *Promoting Children's Mental Health within Early Years and School Settings* is issued by the DfES. It describes indications of risk and resilience and what you can do to help.

WORKING WITH CARERS

● You need to keep in touch with each other. Any major family changes (such as separation, bereavement, even a house move) can upset children for a long while afterwards.

● If you feel that the major cause of the difficulties stems from the situation at home, contact the education social work for advice on family support.

MAKING LINKS

● You might find yourselves working alongside colleagues from social services, Family Support, Services for 'Looked after' children or CAMHS (child and adolescent mental health service).

● Contact your school's education social worker if you need general advice or if you are very concerned about a child's emotional welfare.

● See also the entries on Bereavement (page 15), Family breakdown (page 32), School phobia (page 49) and Separation anxiety (page 55).

Emotional literacy

What you need to know

● There is now a school of thought which claims that there are many different kinds of intelligences, all of which affect our abilities.
● One of these is 'emotional intelligence'. This is a type of social intelligence that involves the ability to monitor one's own and other people's emotions, to discriminate between them, and to use the information to guide one's thinking and actions. It covers self-motivation, empathy, and relationship skills.
● Be aware that some children genuinely find it more difficult than others to understand social situations and handle emotions.
● The term 'emotional literacy' is sometimes used to describe the work you can do with children to foster their mental health and emotional intelligence.
● As the child becomes older, he or she will be encountering more and different types of people in various social situations. Children need emotional literacy skills in order to handle and learn from these situations and to develop as emotional healthy young people.

How to help

● Plan opportunities for the children to talk about the way they feel.
● Help the children to develop a number of words that they can use to describe their own and other people's feelings.
● Help the children to recognise feelings in other people and how they contribute to these.
● Make sure that all of the children feel confident in their school life and enjoy it.
● Teach the children how to be friendly and care for each other.
● Provide ways of controlling their anger and frustration.
● Help the children to develop negotiation skills to solve disputes.
● Teach and support co-operative play.
● Make sure that if a child is feeling anxious, there is a familiar adult or friend at hand to provide reassurance.
● Let the children feel able to make mistakes, and help them to learn from them.
● Look out for natural opportunities throughout the day to make an example of and teach all of these abilities, in the spirit of teaching emotional literacy rather than criticising antisocial behaviour.
● Use circle time approaches to develop the child's sense of identity, to practise social skills and to think about feelings.
● Use a problem solving approach for solving disputes in which the children sit down together and work out what affect the argument is having on each of them and how they can resolve it.

Finding out more

Dealing with Feeling by Tina Rae and *Emotional Literacy Hour* edited by Barbara Maines and Jean Gross (both Lucky Duck Publishing).

WORKING WITH CARERS

● Help parents or carers complete a life story book with their child complete with photographs and drawings if it helps the child make sense of his or her personal history.

MAKING LINKS

● Contact the education social worker if you are concerned about a child's emotional development and want to suggest more support for parents/carers.
See also the page on Semantic pragmatic difficulties (page 51).

Epilepsy

What you need to know

● Some children have recurrent epileptic seizures or 'fits'. These are due to bursts of excessive electrical activity in the brain.

● Seizures can take many forms and vary from child to child. The type of seizure depends on the part of the brain in which these bursts start and spread to.

● About one person in 200 is affected and with varying severity.

● Medical investigations can often lead to medication which helps to control the epilepsy. These children have to be monitored by doctors as they grow older and their condition changes.

● Many children with epilepsy will grow out of it.

● Some children have 'generalised seizures' in which their bodies stiffen, they may cry out, fall and then convulse. These usually last a few minutes and the child may be drowsy and disorientated afterwards.

● Others may look blank, twitch slightly or blink for a few seconds. These may be difficult to spot if you are not familiar with the child.

● Other children may have 'myoclonic seizures' in which a limb or set of muscles jerks for a while, sometimes leading to a fall.

● Children can also experience 'partial seizures' in which they might repeat a behaviour or mannerism, wander or appear unresponsive. These last for 30 seconds to two minutes or so, and the child remains conscious.

How to help

● Make sure you know at what stage any emergency treatment should be sought, for example if a seizure lasts two minutes longer than is usual for that child, or if the child begins to have another seizure before recovering from the first.

● If a child not known to have epilepsy has a seizure, call an ambulance immediately.

● If a child is having a seizure, protect them from injury by cushioning the head and placing the child on their side so that they can breathe easily. Do not restrict their movements or give them anything to drink. Stay with them until they have recovered.

● You will need to handle the seizure where it happens, so have a helper reassure other children and draw them away to an activity.

● If a child is having a partial seizure, lead them gently away from any danger and talk quietly to reassure them.

Finding out more

The British Epilepsy Association/Epilepsy Action can be contacted at New Anstey House, Gate Way Drive, Yeadon, Leeds, LS19 7XY (0808 800 5050), www.epilepsy.org.uk.

WORKING WITH CARERS

● If a child has epilepsy, ask parents/carers to describe what might happen and what you should do. Ask them to stay with their child for the first few sessions to indicate if there are regular seizures.

● Ask if there is anything in particular which might trigger attacks.

● Find out from parents/carers and school nurse about medication and how, when and by whom it should be administered.

MAKING LINKS

● If a child's epilepsy is currently being assessed by the paediatrician or neurologist, you might be able to help by keeping a diary of seizures or unusual mannerisms.

Family breakdown

What you need to know
● At least one in four families in the UK has one parent absent, and in 90% of these families, it is the father. About one child in eight is likely to experience family divorce before the age of ten, and about a third of families are affected by breakdown or new family partners.
● For some children, a family breakdown may be a fact of life. For others, feelings will still be raw and sensitive, and you will need to plan how best to support that child through the next few months.
● Children adjust best to the change if they continue to feel loved and valued by both parents/carers, even though they live apart. Children whose parents/carers discuss with them what is going on tend to cope better. They need information delivered in a way they can understand.

How to help
● Try to understand what family breakdown means from the child's point of view. A family breakdown can take them utterly by surprise and can cause misery and bewilderment. Coming at a time when the parents/carers will be absorbed in their own conflicts and emotions, this can leave the child feeling isolated, and even in some way responsible for the split.
● Make sure that school is an important 'constant' at a time when home life might be confusing and unsettled. Keep to your familiar routines and make allowances if the child wants to work with very familiar or less demanding activities for a while.
● Some children may be feeling very miserable or cross. Others may behave as if nothing is wrong, but may show a reaction later or may show you through their behaviour that they are unsettled. Make allowances for difficult behaviour and stay calm and reassuring as you handle it firmly and consistently, but carefully too.
● Concentrate on making the child feel secure and comforted during the school day.
● If a child is very upset, arrange for a quiet time doing a personalised art or creative writing activity to work through some of the feelings.

Finding out more
Send for some 'Divorce and Separation' leaflets from the *Understanding Childhood* series, The Child Psychotherapy Trust, Star House, 104–108 Grafton Road, London NW5 4BD, www.childpsychotherapytrust.org.uk.

WORKING WITH CARERS
● At school, it will be helpful for you to gather the facts from the parent or carer, and establish what the child knows. Agree the factual information you may need to give the child, and agree one adult in school who is going to be giving particular support to the child.
● Make sure you know who has parental responsibility for the child so that you can keep them informed and consulted about their child's progress.

MAKING LINKS
● The local education social work service should be able to give you more information about 'parental responsibility' and your obligations to keep in touch with separated parents/carers.
● See also 'Emotional difficulties' (page 29).

Dyslexia

What you need to know

● Dyslexia is present when fluent and accurate reading and/or spelling does not develop or does so very incompletely or with great difficulty. This is despite all the usual teaching methods, so you would not usually speak in terms of 'dyslexia' unless various interventions had been tried first.

● It is often referred to as a 'specific learning difficulty' since the level of attainments in literacy skills are much lower than one might predict from the child's intellectual ability or general oral ability.

● The majority of children with dyslexia are boys. The condition appears to run in families, but this is not always the case.

● Main problems are usually one or several of: poor sequencing skills, poor auditory discrimination and memory, poor visual discrimination and memory or poor short-term memory.

● It is important to recognise learning difficulties so that additional time can be granted in exams.

How to help

● Let the child sit where you can provide help unobtrusively.

● Do not expect quite as much written work or homework and allow more time for copying off the board. Encourage oral responses and praise strengths.

● Provide spelling aids (such as the ACE dictionary, available from LDA, or the Franklin Literacy Wordbank, available from John Lewis and www.database2000.co.uk).

● Encourage other uses of ICT, such as editing tools and spell checks.

● Let the child use different forms of presenting their work, such as via mind maps, bullet-point notes or even by recording their voice.

● Break written tasks into smaller steps and help the child organise work before it is begun.

● Do not insist that the child reads out loud.

● Use multi-sensory teaching approaches that allow you to use strengths to support weaknesses.

● Provide enlarged photocopies of worksheets that carry a lot of close text – this makes them easier to use.

● If there is a lot of copying to be done, provide a photocopy of the text to keep instead. Encourage highlighting to mark important points.

● Try to avoid a sense of failure so that the child is not frustrated. Encourage the child to present their creativity in other ways.

● Talk to the SENCO if small group or individual tuition is necessary.

● Teach study skills and mind mapping.

Finding out more

The British Dyslexia Association is at 98 London Road, Reading, RG1 5AU (www.bda-dyslexia.org.uk). Contact The Dyslexia Institute at Park House, Wick Road, Egham, Surrey, TW20 OHH (www.dyslexia-inst.org.uk) for details of assessment/tuition centres.

WORKING WITH CARERS

● Ask parents or carers to have an up to date eye check if visual scanning is a problem, preferably with an orthoptist.

MAKING LINKS

● If a child is receiving private dyslexia tuition, try to make contact with the tutor so that you can work together.
You will find a mention of dyscalculia on the page covering specific learning difficulties (page 56).

Eczema

What you need to know

● Some children have a very itchy, dry, scaly, red rash on their face, their neck, their hands and in the creases of their limbs. For some children, this is widespread and can be debilitating. For others, there are just sore or irritating patches. This is 'eczema' and is a very common allergic reaction. It tends to run in families who suffer from hay fever and asthma.

● Some children have the condition so severely that they are in constant discomfort. It can come and go in severity with good spells and bad spells, sometimes related to the time of year.

● The most common form (atopic eczema) typically develops in the first few months and most children do grow out of it by the time they are around three. By the time they start school, most children's eczema will have improved.

● Eczema can be triggered by certain foods (such as dairy products, eggs or wheat). An attack can also be set off by stress. It may be caused by skin irritants such as wool, washing detergents or pet fur.

How to help

● Find out about any special diet. You may need to ask parents/carers to send in a special snack for their child or some soya milk instead of your usual supply.

● Ask if there is anything that their child cannot handle. For example, some find working with clay difficult as it can dry the skin. Others need to wash hands after handling certain craft materials.

● Washing hands a lot can dry them out, so help the child to dry his or her hands thoroughly and ask parents/carers about a moisturising cream if this will help.

● Do not let your concern show itself as anxiety. If a child is irritated and upset by their condition, they need you to stay calm and to distract them as far as possible.

● Children who have severe eczema can be exhausted in school because of disturbed nights. Sometimes, you may have to provide somewhere for a tired child to rest.

● Use distraction to discourage scratching and rubbing.

● Be flexible about any school uniform so that the child can be comfortable and any affected limbs are covered. A loose cotton tracksuit is usually best for PE.

● Pay attention to room temperature – heat or cold can be uncomfortable for a child with severe eczema. If a child is uncomfortable during PE, make sure there is an open window or fan that any child can use to have a cool down.

Finding out more

Ask your local health visitor or GP for pamphlets about the condition, or visit the National Eczema Organisation's website, www.eczema.org.

WORKING WITH CARERS

● Find out from parents/carers whether there are known triggers for their child's eczema. It may be that you need to avoid physical contact with pets, or make sure they do not handle certain materials.

● Encourage parents and carers to keep the child's nails short and clean to reduce scratching and infection.

MAKING LINKS

● If you have a child with very severe eczema due to attend your class, consider asking their health visitor or school nurse to advise you on their care and any particular precautions you need to take.

Emotional difficulties

What you need to know

● Emotional difficulties in children can take many forms and can stem from many sources. It is most important to address these early in order to prevent mental health problems developing in adulthood.

● Sometimes children seem extremely shy and continue to cry or to be withdrawn long after you feel they should have settled with you.

● Others cannot seem to cope with newness, with failure or with correction. They might destroy their own work or creations as if they did not matter and behave as if they were not bothered by your praise and encouragement.

● Some older children may attempt to harm themselves, to bully others or to abuse substances.

How to help

● Think about the child's self-esteem (page 50) and about ways in which you can encourage and support him or her. Perhaps the child is feeling under pressure in some way. Can you think of anything that would help this? Can you perhaps expect a little less of them for a while, and boost their confidence as much as possible?

● If the child suddenly becomes very anxious and quiet, or behaves in a completely different way (and seems unable to tell you why), then you should talk with parents/carers to try to get to the bottom of it. Remember the child protection procedures (page 19).

● Having predictable routines, clear boundaries for behaviour and familiar people in their lives generally makes children feel more secure.

● Use circle time approaches to help all the children develop self-confidence, a positive self-image and good looking and listening skills.

● If you suspect bullying is going on, consider adopting a problem-solving approach that addresses the issue but also teaches the children to become more sensitive in their dealings with each other. *Crying for help: The no blame approach to bullying* by George Robinson and Barbara Maines (Lucky Duck Publishing) provides useful suggestions.

● Make sure you cover issues such as appropriate assertiveness, bullying and substance abuse as part of your personal and social education curriculum.

Finding out more

The publication *Promoting Children's Mental Health within Early Years and School Settings* is issued by the DfES. It describes indications of risk and resilience and what you can do to help.

SPECIAL NEEDS in the primary years

E

WORKING WITH CARERS

● You need to keep in touch with each other. Any major family changes (such as separation, bereavement, even a house move) can upset children for a long while afterwards.

● If you feel that the major cause of the difficulties stems from the situation at home, contact the education social work for advice on family support.

MAKING LINKS

● You might find yourselves working alongside colleagues from social services, Family Support, Services for 'Looked after' children or CAMHS (child and adolescent mental health service).

● Contact your school's education social worker if you need general advice or if you are very concerned about a child's emotional welfare.

● See also the entries on Bereavement (page 15), Family breakdown (page 32), School phobia (page 49) and Separation anxiety (page 55).

Emotional literacy

What you need to know

● There is now a school of thought which claims that there are many different kinds of intelligences, all of which affect our abilities.
● One of these is 'emotional intelligence'. This is a type of social intelligence that involves the ability to monitor one's own and other people's emotions, to discriminate between them, and to use the information to guide one's thinking and actions. It covers self-motivation, empathy, and relationship skills.
● Be aware that some children genuinely find it more difficult than others to understand social situations and handle emotions.
● The term 'emotional literacy' is sometimes used to describe the work you can do with children to foster their mental health and emotional intelligence.
● As the child becomes older, he or she will be encountering more and different types of people in various social situations. Children need emotional literacy skills in order to handle and learn from these situations and to develop as emotional healthy young people.

How to help

● Plan opportunities for the children to talk about the way they feel.
● Help the children to develop a number of words that they can use to describe their own and other people's feelings.
● Help the children to recognise feelings in other people and how they contribute to these.
● Make sure that all of the children feel confident in their school life and enjoy it.
● Teach the children how to be friendly and care for each other.
● Provide ways of controlling their anger and frustration.
● Help the children to develop negotiation skills to solve disputes.
● Teach and support co-operative play.
● Make sure that if a child is feeling anxious, there is a familiar adult or friend at hand to provide reassurance.
● Let the children feel able to make mistakes, and help them to learn from them.
● Look out for natural opportunities throughout the day to make an example of and teach all of these abilities, in the spirit of teaching emotional literacy rather than criticising antisocial behaviour.
● Use circle time approaches to develop the child's sense of identity, to practise social skills and to think about feelings.
● Use a problem solving approach for solving disputes in which the children sit down together and work out what affect the argument is having on each of them and how they can resolve it.

Finding out more

Dealing with Feeling by Tina Rae and *Emotional Literacy Hour* edited by Barbara Maines and Jean Gross (both Lucky Duck Publishing).

WORKING WITH CARERS
● Help parents or carers complete a life story book with their child complete with photographs and drawings if it helps the child make sense of his or her personal history.

MAKING LINKS
● Contact the education social worker if you are concerned about a child's emotional development and want to suggest more support for parents/carers.
See also the page on Semantic pragmatic difficulties (page 51).

Epilepsy

What you need to know

● Some children have recurrent epileptic seizures or 'fits'. These are due to bursts of excessive electrical activity in the brain.

● Seizures can take many forms and vary from child to child. The type of seizure depends on the part of the brain in which these bursts start and spread to.

● About one person in 200 is affected and with varying severity.

● Medical investigations can often lead to medication which helps to control the epilepsy. These children have to be monitored by doctors as they grow older and their condition changes.

● Many children with epilepsy will grow out of it.

● Some children have 'generalised seizures' in which their bodies stiffen, they may cry out, fall and then convulse. These usually last a few minutes and the child may be drowsy and disorientated afterwards.

● Others may look blank, twitch slightly or blink for a few seconds. These may be difficult to spot if you are not familiar with the child.

● Other children may have 'myoclonic seizures' in which a limb or set of muscles jerks for a while, sometimes leading to a fall.

● Children can also experience 'partial seizures' in which they might repeat a behaviour or mannerism, wander or appear unresponsive. These last for 30 seconds to two minutes or so, and the child remains conscious.

How to help

● Make sure you know at what stage any emergency treatment should be sought, for example if a seizure lasts two minutes longer than is usual for that child, or if the child begins to have another seizure before recovering from the first.

● If a child not known to have epilepsy has a seizure, call an ambulance immediately.

● If a child is having a seizure, protect them from injury by cushioning the head and placing the child on their side so that they can breathe easily. Do not restrict their movements or give them anything to drink. Stay with them until they have recovered.

● You will need to handle the seizure where it happens, so have a helper reassure other children and draw them away to an activity.

● If a child is having a partial seizure, lead them gently away from any danger and talk quietly to reassure them.

Finding out more

The British Epilepsy Association/Epilepsy Action can be contacted at New Anstey House, Gate Way Drive, Yeadon, Leeds, LS19 7XY (0808 800 5050), www.epilepsy.org.uk.

WORKING WITH CARERS

● If a child has epilepsy, ask parents/carers to describe what might happen and what you should do. Ask them to stay with their child for the first few sessions to indicate if there are regular seizures.

● Ask if there is anything in particular which might trigger attacks.

● Find out from parents/carers and school nurse about medication and how, when and by whom it should be administered.

MAKING LINKS

● If a child's epilepsy is currently being assessed by the paediatrician or neurologist, you might be able to help by keeping a diary of seizures or unusual mannerisms.

Family breakdown

What you need to know

● At least one in four families in the UK has one parent absent, and in 90% of these families, it is the father. About one child in eight is likely to experience family divorce before the age of ten, and about a third of families are affected by breakdown or new family partners.

● For some children, a family breakdown may be a fact of life. For others, feelings will still be raw and sensitive, and you will need to plan how best to support that child through the next few months.

● Children adjust best to the change if they continue to feel loved and valued by both parents/carers, even though they live apart. Children whose parents/carers discuss with them what is going on tend to cope better. They need information delivered in a way they can understand.

How to help

● Try to understand what family breakdown means from the child's point of view. A family breakdown can take them utterly by surprise and can cause misery and bewilderment. Coming at a time when the parents/carers will be absorbed in their own conflicts and emotions, this can leave the child feeling isolated, and even in some way responsible for the split.

● Make sure that school is an important 'constant' at a time when home life might be confusing and unsettled. Keep to your familiar routines and make allowances if the child wants to work with very familiar or less demanding activities for a while.

● Some children may be feeling very miserable or cross. Others may behave as if nothing is wrong, but may show a reaction later or may show you through their behaviour that they are unsettled. Make allowances for difficult behaviour and stay calm and reassuring as you handle it firmly and consistently, but carefully too.

● Concentrate on making the child feel secure and comforted during the school day.

● If a child is very upset, arrange for a quiet time doing a personalised art or creative writing activity to work through some of the feelings.

Finding out more

Send for some 'Divorce and Separation' leaflets from the *Understanding Childhood* series, The Child Psychotherapy Trust, Star House, 104–108 Grafton Road, London NW5 4BD, www.childpsychotherapytrust.org.uk.

WORKING WITH CARERS

● At school, it will be helpful for you to gather the facts from the parent or carer, and establish what the child knows. Agree the factual information you may need to give the child, and agree one adult in school who is going to be giving particular support to the child.

● Make sure you know who has parental responsibility for the child so that you can keep them informed and consulted about their child's progress.

MAKING LINKS

● The local education social work service should be able to give you more information about 'parental responsibility' and your obligations to keep in touch with separated parents/carers.

● See also 'Emotional difficulties' (page 29).

Family therapy

What you need to know

● Occasionally, you may have a child in your school who is attending family therapy sessions with members of their family.

● Sometimes this is related to a problem you already know about, for example a behavioural problem or emotional difficulty in one of the children.

● Difficult behaviours or emotional problems can have complex causes, and it sometimes makes sense for a specialist to work with the whole family. This might be to work on their expectations and relationships and to help them pull together as a family unit, yet value each other as individuals.

● At other times, you may not understand why they are attending, as the reasons are confidential and do not concern the school. Perhaps there was a bereavement long ago that is affecting how members of the family handle day-to-day situations now.

● Most family therapy sessions are conducted by a therapist and co-therapist, often with other professionals observing and making suggestions. There are different models of therapy which different teams adopt.

● Usually the whole family is seen together, occasionally with extended family members as well.

● Be aware that to gain full benefit, families will usually have to attend for several sessions.

How to help

● If a child is absent from school for regular family therapy sessions, please try to support this by providing opportunities for the child to catch up on missed activities or to just to play quietly for a while if the child seems unsettled afterwards.

● Sometimes children's behaviour may be unsettled or excitable after a session, because of sensitive matters or strong feelings that have arisen. Provide a quiet corner for the child to play through any remaining emotions or allow them to take a lively run outside to spend some energy.

● A family might go through a stage of feeling angry at the therapist and this is sometimes part of the process of pulling together more and it can actually lead to positive change. Try not to worry if this happens – it is not necessarily a sign that things aren't working!

● If parents and carers are feeling rather threatened by the process, commend them for all the work they are doing to help in attending the sessions and doing such a valuable piece of work together. Reassure them that it may not be an easy process, but it is worth trying if the family situation has become 'stuck' for whatever reason.

Finding out more

Read *Helping Families with Troubled Children* by Carole Sutton (Wiley).

WORKING WITH CARERS

● Reassure parents or carers that they should find the session challenging but helpful.

● Offer (through parents/carers) to work with the therapists by sending information or planning special activities for the child if this would help.

MAKING LINKS

● Family therapy services can usually be found within the NHS CAMHS ('Child and Adolescent Mental Health Service') Teams, in social services and also in certain Voluntary Organisations. See also the entry on Play therapy (page 46).

Hearing impairment

What you need to know

● Many young children suffer from temporary, fluctuating or even permanent hearing loss.

● About 840 children a year are born with a permanent hearing impairment, and thousands more will have a temporary loss.

● Temporary hearing loss can be caused by colds that have led to ear infections. Other children have a build up of mucus in the middle ear which stops sounds being transmitted properly and can lead to conductive deafness. This is known as glue ear and is often treated at hospital by draining the mucus and inserting grommets. 'Sensori-neural deafness' usually means that sounds are not being processed correctly in the inner ear. This can follow rubella, mumps or meningitis and is likely to be a permanent hearing impairment.

● In 'mixed deafness', children may have a mixture of conductive and sensori-neural hearing impairment. Very few children are totally deaf.

● Some children need hearing aids to amplify sound. Cochlear implants are a kind of hearing aid that send electrical signals to the brain. Radio aids help you communicate clearly to the child even if there is background noise.

● Some children are taught to use signs as an aid to communicating clearly as well as understanding. Others learn to lip-read or to follow as many clues as possible using 'total communication'.

How to help

● You are in a good position to identify hearing difficulty early on. Early identification is vital, as it can affect language development.

● Make sure you have the child's attention before speaking. Keep in front of them and at the same level, or slightly to the side if the child has a greater hearing loss in one ear.

● Minimise background noise by using soft surfaces to absorb sound.

● Make sure that spaces are well lit so faces can be seen clearly. Speak clearly and slowly, and do not shout.

● Keep up to date with any signs the child might be using, so that you can use and understand these and clarify what is being said. Share this knowledge with colleagues, including non-teaching staff.

● Be aware that new sounds (such as a loud musical instrument or a fire alarm practice) might be unpleasant or even painful for some children's ears. Warn the child in advance if at all possible.

Finding out more

RNID have useful publications for teachers and families Contact the Royal National Institute for Deaf People, 0808 808 01 23 or visit their website, www.rnid.org.uk.

WORKING WITH CARERS

● Speak with the parents/carers and health visitor if you have concerns about a child's hearing, even if the loss seems to be intermittent.

MAKING LINKS

● Contact your local service for Hearing Impaired Children through the LEA Support Service. See also 'Disability Act' (page 25) and 'Inclusion' (page 37).

HIV/AIDS

What you need to know
● AIDS is caused by the HIV virus (Human Immunodeficiency Virus) which can damage the body's defence system.
● Blood tests can be used to detect whether a person is HIV-positive (carrying the HIV virus). People who are HIV-positive usually go on to develop AIDS at some point, though the time scale is variable and new medications are developing all the time.
● It is transmitted by an exchange of fluids. For example, an unborn child might acquire the virus from an infected mother.
● Improved medication has helped greatly to improve the life expectancy of babies born to HIV-positive mothers. It can take as long as 10 to 15 years for HIV to destroy the immune system.
● Young children are not likely to feel that there is anything wrong unless they start to become chronically ill.
● Children who know they are HIV-positive often instinctively keep quiet about this. Some may want to talk to someone outside the family about it and others will not.
● Children with HIV only pose a small risk to others, though they may themselves be prone to infections from others. There is no evidence that HIV can be transmitted by everyday social contact, cuddles, coughs, sneezes, tears, saliva or sharing a toilet seat.

How to help
● Inform yourself fully about HIV and AIDS. This will help you to avoid becoming over-protective either to a child with HIV or to the other children.
● Take sensible precautions whenever dealing with bleeding incidents for *all* children. Wear protective gloves and dispose of all blood and bodily fluid products safely.
● Normal everyday standards of good hygiene are quite sufficient. Follow the First Aid and Health & Safety guidelines of your particular school or Authority.
● Do all you can to keep the general health of the children as strong as possible (through healthy eating, rest and exercise). This helps to strengthen their immune systems.
● Maintain confidentiality; parents/carers are not obliged to tell you if their child has HIV. Operate a 'need to know' policy in school.
● Warn all parents/carers about any virulent infections going round, such as measles or chicken pox.

Finding out more
The Terence Higgins Trust: 52–54 Grays Inn Road, London WC1X 8JU. Helpline: 0845 122 12 00; website: www.tht.org.uk
Barnardo's, Tanners Lane, Barkingside, Ilford. IG6 1QG. www.barnardos.org.uk. The booklet *AIDS in the Family* is jointly produced by these two organisations.

WORKING WITH CARERS
● You may not be told that a child has HIV though many parents/carers tell at least one member of staff so that they can be alerted about particular infections in the school.
● Remember that parents may have their own health problems and need your extra understanding and support as well.

MAKING LINKS
● Build up a resource library for colleagues and parents/carers so that everyone becomes better informed about the condition. Share accurate information and try to expel any myths and misunderstandings.

IEP

What you need to know

● Individual education plans should be a key feature of planning for any SEN in your school either as part of your School Action (page 47) or your School Action Plus (page 48).

● They should contain three or four short-term targets and make it clear how you will know that your teaching has been successful.

● They should lead to the child making progress and should be seen as an integrated aspect of the curriculum planning for the whole class.

● You should be differentiating the curriculum for a range of individual needs anyway, so an IEP need only include that which is additional to or different from the regular curriculum that is in place for all of the children.

● When children have common targets (and common teaching strategies) in a class, it is possible to write a group education plan.

WORKING WITH CARERS

● IEPs need to be reviewed with parents or carers at least twice a year and should clearly show the help which parents and carers have agreed to put in as well.

MAKING LINKS

● Your SENCO or will be able to provide you with help and support on writing IEPs and putting them into practice.

● If you are monitoring the child's needs at 'school action plus', then there will also be an outside professional (such as a learning support teacher or educational psychologist) who can guide you.

● See also 'School Action' (page 47).

How to help

● There is no set format, and you need to design an IEP that is clear, accessible and understandable for your school. The SENCO will advise you on the best format to use.

● You might include: the name of the child, whether you are planning School Action or School Action Plus, the nature of the child's difficulty, a list of the child's strengths, the action you are planning and who will do what, the help which will come from parents or carers, three or four targets for the term, your monitoring and assessment arrangements, when you will review the IEP with parents/carers and who else you will invite to the review meeting.

● Targets should be 'SMART'- specific, measurable, achievable, realistic and time bound, for example 'By the end of this term, Aston will be able to write a short paragraph of independent prose, coming to me for difficult spellings'.

● The IEP should underpin all of your planning and intervention for the child with learning difficulties and should therefore be shared with colleagues, parents and carers.

● It must include *what* should be taught, *how* it should be taught and *how often* the additional or different provision will be made.

● Use the IEP to show how you will differentiate (break down) your activities in order to make the curriculum accessible to those children who have SEN.

Finding out more

You will find examples of individual education plans in other books in this series, in particular the *Special Needs Handbook*.

Inclusion

What you need to know
● The idea of 'inclusion' is now firmly embedded within the SEN Code of Practice (page 20) and the SEN Disability Act (page 25).
● When children with SEN used to be 'integrated' into mainstream provision, they used to attend their local school *if they could cope.* Inclusion goes much further – they attend their local school *because they are there.* Only if it is proved that their needs cannot be met might a more specialist placement be sought.
● Inclusion is a journey and not a destination: each LEA differs in how far their policies have come along that road. However, they are all heading in the same direction.

How to help
● If you are making use of extra adult support for a child with SEN, use careful joint planning to make sure that the child is fully included and has the chance to function as independently as possible.
● Use educational labels rather than categories or medical labels (such as 'co-ordination difficulty' rather than 'dyspraxia', 'a child who has epilepsy' rather than 'epileptic' or 'child who has SEN' rather than 'SEN child').
● Provide good role models for the children because of your positive expectations and the way you respect and value the children.

● Do all that you can to improve children's communication skills, for example, by teaching signing to everyone, or using a communication book to show how a severely disabled child makes his or her needs known.
● Use teaching strategies that enable *all* children to join in the activities and to learn from them.

● Plan individual approaches which are based on pupils' earlier experiences, which set high expectations, and which encourage the children to support each other.
● Plan any extra support flexibly and creatively so that it promotes joining in and inclusion rather than creating barriers and exclusion.
● Often, a teaching activity or lesson can be changed in some way to suit individual needs and you should never exclude certain children from it because they cannot 'fit in' with it.

Finding out more
The Index for Inclusion: Developing Learning and Participation in Schools is published by the CSIE (Centre for Studies on Inclusive Education), New Redland, Frenchay Campus, Coldharbour Lane, Bristol, BS16 1QU. A list of further publications is available on their website: http://inclusion.uwe.ac.uk.

WORKING WITH CARERS
● Gather as much information as you can from parents and carers about a child with disability. This will enable you to set high expectations and build on their strengths whilst supporting their weaknesses.
● Sometimes parents/ carers might wish you to be very protective of their child; establish trust with them first and then work together to achieve a healthy balance between independence and protection.

MAKING LINKS
● Suggest some disability awareness and inclusion training for your school or cluster. For example, contact Disability Equality in Education: Unit GL. Leroy House, 436 Essex Road, London N1 3QP www.diseed.org.uk.

Independence training

What you need to know

● Young children vary greatly in the ages at which they achieve personal independence in areas like getting dressed by themselves, using the toilet or feeding themselves.

● You may notice that some of your older children are still very reliant on a parent or carer to organise them and, as a result, lack initiative and the ability to organise themselves.

● Some strive for independence, even if it is clear that they still need help. Others are quite content to have everything done for them.

● Children who have SEN may have more difficulties than others in acquiring independence, perhaps because their hands are clumsy, they have short attention spans, or they cannot plan ahead so well.

How to help

● When you are planning for SEN, think of the child's future as well as the National Curriculum. Plan for independence, personal, social and emotional skills as well as the standard curriculum areas.

● Learn to provide just the right amount of help, and no more, to the child to whom you are teaching independence skills.

● Allow plenty of time for a child with disabilities to dress or undress independently and stay close to encourage and celebrate success.

● Think ahead about the independence skills necessary for Key Stage 3 (such as personal organisation and time management) and break these down into steps that you can teach before transfer.

● Teach step-by-step and then chain the steps together so that the child is managing more complex tasks.

● Try to give the children choices wherever possible, and set up situations so that they can exercise their ability to be independent.

● Start to encourage different learning styles (visual, auditory, kinaesthetic) and use multi-sensory approaches where appropriate.

● Use Key Stages 1 and 2 to make sure that the children learn how to learn as well as what to learn.

● Introduce multi-sensory study skills (such as mind mapping, mnemonics and thought storming) for all children, and especially those with learning difficulties.

● Think through the independence skills of all the children: toilets need to be accessible and welcoming, wash-basins reachable, craft materials and technology equipment easy to reach and choices given for activities wherever possible.

Finding out more

Find out how to use your ICT equipment to make children with disabilities as independent as possible. Send for a catalogue from KCS, FREEPOST, Southampton SO17 1YA, www.keytools.com. Many LEAs now have a specialist support teacher for children with physical disabilities: contact your local LEA support service.

WORKING WITH CARERS

● Help parents or carers to become familiar with just how much their child can do without help, and just how much help is needed. They should then help those parts of any routine task that need it, but also stand back at the right moment for their child to complete the task "all by myself".

MAKING LINKS

● If a child's self-help skills are affected by their disability, the paediatric occupational therapist at the local hospital might be able to advise you.

● These professionals can also advise you on adaptations, suitable aids and special equipment, such as specialist scissors, tools, writing resources, and so on.

Learning difficulties

What you need to know
● These are the legal definitions given in the 1996 Education Act (Section 312) and would be useful for you to know.
● A child is described as having 'special educational needs' if he or she has a 'learning difficulty' which needs 'special educational provision' to be made for him or her.
● A child has a 'learning difficulty' if he or she has a difficulty in learning that is significantly different from the majority of children of the same age, or has a disability which prevents or hinders them from making use of educational facilities of a kind usually provided for children of the same age in schools within the area of the LEA.
● In practice, 'special educational provision' means that you are having to provide support that is *additional* and *different* to usual.
● Given that your school already has to be flexible enough to meet the needs of a wide range of individual needs, you are only likely to be deciding they have SEN if they are functioning (approximately) more than one year outside of their typical age for whatever reason (be it academic learning, physical development, language and communication or social behaviour).

How to help
● Sometimes the reason for a child's learning difficulty is known; perhaps there is a diagnosis or a recognised disability. In other cases, it appears that they are simply developing more slowly. You do not always need to know the reason to be able to support and help them.
● Instead, use your methods of observation and assessment to work out the child's strengths and weaknesses and take School Action (page 47) to address their needs.
● Break learning activities down to make your teaching more accessible to the child so that they can take as full a part as possible in your curriculum. The SENCO can advise you on how you can use differentiation effectively in your classroom.
● Where appropriate, use any additional support flexibly – perhaps viewing it as an extra pair of hands which releases you to work alongside a child for a short time.

Finding out more
MENCAP, www.mencap.org.uk is a support organisation for children with severe learning difficulties and their families.

WORKING WITH CARERS
● Coming to terms with the fact that their child has learning difficulties can be a distressing time for parents and carers. Try to tune into the feelings of disbelief, anger, sorrow, guilt or protectiveness that they might be feeling. If their reaction to you is defensive or 'prickly', try not to take this personally.

MAKING LINKS
● If you feel that you need more specialist assessment and advice, then discuss this with the SENCO and consider planning School Action Plus' (page 48).
● Reassure parents and carers that taking School Action Plus (page 48) need not mean that there is something seriously wrong with the child – it simply needs that *you* all need more advice and support to meet their particular needs.

WORKING WITH CARERS

● Talk with parents/carers if medication is needed in school. There is no legal duty on you to administer medication, however, it can affect whether or not a child can attend your school.
● Have procedures for keeping medicines safe, recording information about dosage and signing when it has been administered.
● Children with serious medical difficulties usually have a specialist paediatric nurse who knows their condition well. Contact parents/carers or the local Children's Ward for information.

MAKING LINKS

● If a child is spending long or frequent periods in hospital, make contact with the hospital teacher.
● See also 'Asthma' (page 12), 'Cancer and leukaemia' (page 17), 'Cystic fibrosis (page 21), 'Diabetes' (page 25), 'Eczema' (page 28), 'Epilepsy', (page 31), 'HIV/AIDS' (page 35) and 'Meningitis' (opposite).

Medical difficulties

What you need to know

● About 10 to 15 per cent of children under 16 are affected by chronic, long-term physical or medical problems. The most common conditions are eczema (eight to ten per cent of children), asthma (two to five per cent), diabetes (1.8 per cent), congenital heart disease and epilepsy (both about 0.5 per cent).
● There are other potentially frightening or painful conditions and many of these have an unpredictable course, including sickle cell anaemia, rheumatoid arthritis, HIV infections and AIDS (page 35), cystic fibrosis (page 21), cancer and leukaemia (page 17).
● Once children begin to understand that they are ill, they will still not know much about their condition; more about what it means *to them*. They will add to and modify this understanding as they grow older.

How to help

● Collect all the information you need from parents, carers and health professionals. You need to know what the medical condition means for the child, what it means for you and what to look out for.
● When talking about a child's medical condition, concentrate on the here and now. Help the child find words for how they are feeling, what is happening and what will happen next. Keep this information factual and correct, relating it in practical terms to what it means for the child.
● Impending visits to hospital and clinics can be frightening until a child understands exactly what will happen. Talk with parents or carers if this is the case and use regular talking times to help.
● Young children make sense of their world by mastering the familiar routines and rules that form their day. You can help younger children in the classroom by keeping routines as familiar as possible. Provide opportunities for older children to talk and write about themselves if they feel ready to.
● Make links between home and school, or with hospital or hospice, to keep familiar activities and contacts going during absence.

Finding out more

The DfES publication *Supporting Pupils with Medical Needs* is available from www.teachernet.gov.uk. The *Contact a Family Directory* can be obtained on subscription from 'Contact a Family', 170 Tottenham Court Road, London. W1P 0HA. The Contact a Family website (www.cafamily.org.uk) may also be useful.

Meningitis

What you need to know

● 'Meningitis' literally means 'inflammation of the meninges', which is the membrane lining the brain and the spinal cord.

● It can be caused by different germs, and severity depends on the germ involved. Early symptoms usually look the same to a layperson.

● Bacterial meningitis is quite rare, with around 2000 reported cases a year in the UK. However, it can be very serious and needs urgent treatment with antibiotics.

● Viral meningitis is more common and is rarely life threatening, but can make the sufferer feel very weak and unwell. Antibiotics are not effective, so this is usually treated with nursing, rest and care.

● The germs can be spread by coughing, sneezing and very close contact, but do not survive for long outside the body. They are not likely to be passed through handling tools and equipment, though good hygiene practice, especially with mouthed musical instruments, should always be followed.

● Symptoms look like flu to begin with – fever, vomiting, headache, and a marked stiffness, particularly at the back of the neck.

● The child finds bright light painful, might complain of joint stiffness, and, in time, becomes drowsy. Sometimes the child develops fits and a widespread blotchy rash or bruising associated with blood poisoning (septicaemia). Usually this rash does not disappear when you press a transparent glass against the skin.

● The illness sometimes develops over one or two days, but can come on very quickly in a manner of a few hours. In these cases, it becomes clear very soon that the child is very ill indeed and emergency treatment should be sought.

How to help

● Make sure you and your colleagues are aware of the symptoms of meningitis and take immediate action if you suspect that a child might be affected. Contact parents or carers and arrange an immediate visit to the GP or Accident and Emergency department. If the child is difficult to rouse, send for an ambulance immediately.

● Children recovering from viral meningitis can feel weak, debilitated and depressed for some time. They may feel floppy, tired and irritable and need patience and reassurance for several weeks.

● New topics might have been lost and need to be retaught.

● Just occasionally, there are effects which are longer term. Monitor the child's learning, attention, concentration, emotional response and behaviour for a while after recovery and share any concerns with parents/carers and doctors if you suspect long-term changes.

Finding out more

Local health clinics, hospitals and GP surgeries carry pamphlets. Have plenty of these at school in waiting areas and staffrooms.

WORKING WITH CARERS

● Keep a particular note of the child's hearing after meningitis since this may well have been affected and you will need to request an up-to-date check from parents/carers.

● Your school doctor will advise you on any letters you need to send out to all parents/carers if there is meningitis in your locality or school.

MAKING LINKS

● If a child has been hospitalised for some time, make contact with the hospital teacher to see whether it would be appropriate to send in some suitable activities to pass the time.

Multiple difficulties

What you need to know

● Some children are profoundly disabled in all areas of their development and learning. They may have been described as having 'profound and multiple learning difficulties'.

● Sometimes, difficulties arise because of brain injury around birth or some other trauma. Something may have gone wrong with their development very early in pregnancy, affecting the way in which their bodies and brains developed, or perhaps there is a chromosomal abnormality or other syndrome associated with profound developmental delay.

● There can be enormous benefits from meeting the child's needs in an inclusive primary school, so long as their needs have been carefully assessed, everybody works as a team, and he or she can be supported appropriately.

● Usually, these children will have a 'statement of special educational needs' from the LEA, describing their needs and the resources needed to meet those needs.

How to help

● The child is likely to have a special support assistant allocated for their care. Try not to regard this person as 'the expert' but share the care and encouragement for the child across all colleagues so that you all learn develop skills in meeting the child's multiple needs.

● Talk to parents or carers about how the child makes their needs known. How do they know when their child is tired, upset, hungry, happy? Put together a communication book with photographs of the child and what their various expressions and behaviours mean. This can then be shared with all colleagues.

● You may need a quiet corner for some peace and if the child indicates that he or she is sleepy.

● Look for activities where the child can feel and touch things and can enjoy interacting with others. Even if you are teaching something using words and pictures, find something that the child can explore on a sensory and tactile level.

● Demonstrate appropriate ways in which other children can interact with the child and help them to tune in with the child's responses.

● You may find the P scales helpful in planning the curriculum for a child with multiple difficulties. These are early goals which can be used for effective target setting for pupils with SEN. Send for the document *Supporting the Target Setting Process* (DfES 0065/2001).

Finding out more

Assessing communication in the classroom by Clare Latham and Ann Miles (David Fulton Publishers) helps you plan for the communication of pupils with profound and multiple learning difficulties.

WORKING WITH CARERS

● Make a special welcome to the parents and carers who might have had a difficult time coming to terms with their child's condition. ● It will be an anxious time whilst they see how their child is coping in your class, and whether you are coping with their child's needs.

MAKING LINKS

● Find out which other professionals are involved so that you can share approaches and seek advice on 'next steps' to encourage. There is probably a local Child Development Centre Team involved or a team of therapists from the paediatric department of the local hospital. They can advise you on handling, developmental teaching and day-to-day caring.

Parent supporters

What you need to know

● The revised SEN Code of Practice has strengthened the role and the rights that parents and carers have when their child has (or is being assessed for) SEN.

● LEAs have a statutory duty to ensure that parents and carers of children with SEN are given advice about those needs.

● Most LEAs appoint Parent Partnership Officers to offer advice and support parents/carers at any stage of the SEN process.

● They work alongside schools, educational psychologists, support teachers, education social workers and other professionals but are also able to give independent advice.

● They can listen to parents'/carers' worries and concerns, explain the assessment processes to them and help them have their say or develop their input.

● There are also 'independent parental supporters' who can support parents/carers through their child's SEN assessment and afterwards.

● When the LEA issues a child's statement, they must inform the parents/carers of somebody who can give advice and information, and tell them the name of the 'Named Officer' of the LEA from whom further information can be obtained.

How to help

● If a parent/carer would like an independent parental supporter whilst their child is being assessed, help them to contact the Parent Partnership Officer at the Education Department.

● It may be possible for them to be introduced to an independent parental supporter through a Parents' Support Group or through a Volunteer Centre. Find out about local voluntary organisations through the local Council for Voluntary Services.

● Explain to parents or carers that many of these independent parental supporters are themselves parets or carers of children with special needs and they have volunteered to support other families.

● Never underestimate the support that you yourselves can offer to the parents or carers of a child who has SEN. You do not need to know all the answers – simply where to find them out.

● Parents/carers in similar situations can offer invaluable support to each other. Seek mutual permission first before passing names on. You might offer your school as a place for a support group to meet.

● Parent Partnership services are also involved in resolving disputes between parents/carers and others where these are related to SEN.

Finding out more

Section 2 of the SEN Code of Practice describes the roles of those who work with parents/carers in the SEN process.

WORKING WITH CARERS

● Parent Partnership Officers can help parents/carers to say what they think their child's needs are and help the child's views to be represented. If there are difficulties or misunderstandings between parents/carers and LEAs, then the Parent Partnership Officer will try to resolve them.

MAKING LINKS

● Parent Partnership services have a responsibility for working with schools to help you develop positive relationships with parents/carers. They can also arrange training for schools.

SPECIAL NEEDS in the primary years

P

Pathological Demand Avoidance

What you need to know
● Pathological Demand Avoidance Syndrome (PDA) is a pervasive developmental disorder identified as a separate syndrome by Professor Elizabeth Newson at the University of Nottingham.
● The syndrome is related to autism (page 14) and Asperger Syndrome (page 11) though these children are more socially skilled and able to manipulate social situations well.
● These children seem almost driven to resist and avoid the normal demands of everyday life. This goes far beyond the kind of resistance you would see from a strong-willed child or a child who is trying to avoid stress or effort. It is a condition that should be diagnosed by a professional rather than a label that you apply yourself.
● Children with PDA lack insight of 'self' and therefore do not see themselves as being responsible or to blame for their actions. They appear to lack pride or shame.
● They are highly motivated to avoid any demands you make of them, using distraction or temper to control the situation.
● It is more than difficult temperament – these children usually have an early history of language delay and being passive as babies.

How to help
● Look for the best balance of keeping the child on task for as long as possible each day, ensuring information learned is retained and ensuring the minimal disruption to other pupils.
● If you have additional support, use a key-worker system to keep the child motivated and 'on task'.
● Be aware that some of these children will 'act' attentive but have not actually learned properly, so check regularly for retention.
● Anxiety about losing control can cause outbursts of temper – treat this as a panic attack rather than aggression and allow the child to calm down somewhere quiet before dealing with the incident.
● Use the 'Circle of Friends' approach with all children to improve support and teach interpersonal understanding.
● Use a variety of strategies, including humour, role-play, patience, indirect requests ('I wonder what the best way to do this is…?')
● Be aware that what works today might not work tomorrow but may well be effective again next week.

Finding out more
The PDA Contact Group is based at 24 Daybrook Road, London SW19 3DH and the website is www.pdacontact.org.uk. *Circle of Friends – Promoting Social Inclusion* by Jackie Lown is available from Positive Behaviour Management, 7 Quinton Close, Ainsdale, Merseyside, PR8 2TD.

WORKING WITH CARERS
● You will each need considerable support and information from the other. Take time to form a close relationship and try to see the difficulty as an incapacity on the part of the child rather than 'naughtiness'.
● If possible, arrange for the child to have 15 minutes of one-to-one counselling or relaxation at the start and end of each school day to make the transfer between schools easier for the child.

MAKING LINKS
● You will probably find yourself working alongside the LEA's behaviour support teacher or an educational psychologist.

Physical difficulties

What you need to know

● Children who have physical and co-ordination difficulties have a wide range of needs. Some might have mobility difficulties and require the use of a wheelchair or walking frame. Others may have 'fine-motor' problems and find it hard to dress, hold a pencil or make small finger movements.

● Sometimes this will be because of a recognised condition such as cerebral palsy (page 18) or spina bifida (page 58).
● Sometimes it will be because their physical development is delayed for their age on account of other developmental difficulties.
● Sometimes they are clumsy and their co-ordination is still immature, perhaps because they have a specific learning difficulty.
● Children with mobility difficulties have the same needs as all children – to learn, to play, to make friends and to access the national curriculum.
● Some children will have been given special equipment to help them sit, stand, move and balance.

How to help

● Try to see your classroom from the point of view of the child with mobility difficulties. Is the floor free from obstacles? Is it comfortable for small groups to sit and work on? Can all activity surfaces (such as computers and workbenches) be accessed by any pupil with mobility difficulties? Is art, technology, science and other equipment accessible for the child with fine motor difficulties? Can the child still make choices and learn independently? Are all your spaces accessible to children in wheelchairs or with rollators? Can they open doors, reach for equipment, join in group activities?
● Know when to stand back and allow the child to be independent. Provide opportunities for learning in different positions; lying, kneeling, sitting or standing at a table.
● Ensure that your reading and reference books and your stories reflect a wide range of ability, including wheelchair-users.

Finding out more

The British Association of Occupational Therapists: 106–114 Borough High Street, Southwark, London SE1 1LB, www.cot.co.uk. Chartered Society of Physiotherapy: 14, Bedford Way, London, WC1R 4ED, www.csp.org.uk. Step-By-Step, 0845 3001089, www.sbs-educational.co.uk, supplies toys for all special needs.

WORKING WITH CARERS

● Use parents/carers as the 'experts' on their child's physical condition and what they need to support them. They can also show you how to use any special equipment.

MAKING LINKS

● Contact the physiotherapist or occupational therapist for advice on equipment, seating and positioning. If you have activities and equipment that you feel is not accessible to everyone, then discuss this with the therapist and seek advice.
● See also 'Cerebral palsy' (page 18), 'Developmental co-ordination difficulty' (page 22) and 'Spina bifida and hydrocephalus' (page 58).

Play therapy

What you need to know

● Children cannot always tell you what is wrong – sometimes they simply don't know, or they lack the words to describe how they feel. However, it is often possible to observe them express their feelings through play. For example, we can observe an older brother or sister playing with dolls and acting out considerable feelings of love, anger or fantasy after the arrival of a new baby in the family.

● Sometimes we can observe the way children play and interpret how they are thinking about their life and what has happened to them. This is helpful for children who are emotionally vulnerable or who have been affected by certain events in their lives.

● Even older children can benefit from spending regular time with a dependable and interested professional who is able to contain their strong feelings as they act and play them out in a therapeutic and emotionally secure environment.

● Over the years, psychologists have developed ways of interpreting children's play and the readiness with which they absorb themselves in 'miniature worlds'. This has led to complex methods of interpreting a child's play and also helping them make sense of their feelings through a method known as play therapy.

How to help

● Because these approaches have evolved following careful research of how young children behave and develop, they should not be used to interpret children's play too loosely. However, you can make good use of the principles, to help all children cope in difficult times.

● For younger children, provide a hospital corner to help children play through any feelings they have about doctors and hospitals.

● Collect children's storybooks about issues such as a new baby, a new family, going to the dentist, death and bereavement, divorce and separation, and moving away.

● Some local library services or toy libraries lend themed books or play packs around these subjects.

● If a child's behaviour suddenly becomes especially violent or unusual in some way, work alongside them and give them the opportunity to share their feelings with you. This might help you understand what has affected the child.

● If a child is attending play therapy sessions at your local centre, be aware that their behaviour might be rather unsettled for a while afterwards. If so, provide a quiet area to 'wind down' for a while before returning to lessons.

Finding out more

The Magination Press (www.maginationpress.com) specialises in books that help children deal with personal or psychological concerns (see page 64).

WORKING WITH CARERS

● Contact parents or carers if the child's play suddenly changes – they may be able to tell you what is happening that might have caused this. Remember the child protection procedures if you have serious concerns about the child's safety (page 19).

MAKING LINKS

● Play therapists are psychologists or therapists usually based in NHS Child and Family Centres. Contact your local CAMHS service or the health visitor for information.

● See also the pages on Emotional difficulties (page 30) and Family therapy (page 33).

School Action

What you need to know
● The SEN Code of Practice asks you to plan the curriculum so that it is accessible for all children, including those who have SEN.
● Many children's SEN will be met simply by your adapting your approaches and targeting the learning more carefully – in other words by your taking 'School Action'.
● Others may require 'School Action Plus' where an outside professional becomes involved (page 48).

How to help
● You have a responsibility for developing your own basic knowledge and skills in supporting pupils with SEN and it is no longer sufficient to consider SEN as the responsibility of 'those more specialised than I am'. The school SENCO should be your source of information.
● Have faith that the interventions you plan really work! Don't feel that if you have identified a child's SEN then it requires an SEN expert to deal with them. You are an expert in how children learn and this is precisely where the child needs support.
● If you feel that a child has SEN, you should gather information about the child from observations, samples of work and assessments.
● You can then plan how to make the learning more accessible to the child by breaking each learning objective into smaller steps or setting easier objectives (differentiation).
● A starting point for differentiation is to look at a child's particular strengths and interests. Choose projects and reading material, for example, which are about something that the child enjoys and are at a level appropriate to the child's stage of language and skills. Include concrete props to hold attention, emphasise meaning and allow a child to participate with more than one sense at once.
● All staff should work closely with the child, following the IEP that has been agreed. They should also observe and record progress, and meet with parents/carers and the SENCO to review progress.
● All curriculum planning will include a degree of planning for different levels of children's ability. Within this, it might be that some children need learning steps broken down more; it may be necessary to give value to a smaller and less obvious learning outcome.
● You might also need to present the activities in a different way using adapted equipment or a more structured teaching situation, perhaps led and supported by a classroom assistant.

Finding out more
Consult *The SEN Code of Practice* (DfES). *Removing Barriers to Achievement: The Government's Strategy for SEN*, available from the DfES and www.teachernet.gov.uk/wholeschool/sen/senstrategy. *The Special Needs Handbook* from this series may be useful.

WORKING WITH CARERS
● Gather information from parents and carers who know the child and use this information to help your planning.
● Parents/carers must always be kept fully informed of their child's progress.

MAKING LINKS
● Each school should have a SEN Co-ordinator (or 'SENCO', page 53) who will develop expertise on SEN, support you all as you meet a child's SEN, and be responsible for liaising with parents and carers and any other professionals.
● See also the pages on Code of Practice for SEN (page 20), IEPs (page 36) and School Action Plus (page 48).

School Action Plus

What you need to know
● Some children with SEN require higher levels of support and differentiation and you might need to bring on board specialist expertise if the child is experiencing continuing difficulties – in other words through planning School Action Plus.
● Specialist advice might be through an educational psychologist, learning or behaviour support teacher, speech and language therapist or others.
● This does not mean that assessment should be seen as a linear process, moving from School Action to School Action Plus. Instead, assessment and intervention should be appropriate to a child's individual needs at any particular time, each review of the process informing and feeding on to the next.
● In practice, you might feel after several reviews that a child is still not making the progress that might be possible. So, you might decide to call in an outside agency for more advice, assessment and support. This advice would then become part of the IEP (page 36).

How to help
● Usually, a request for help from outside agencies is likely to follow a decision taken by SENCO, colleagues and parents/carers when reviewing a child's progress in school. Has progress been made? What do parents/carers feel? Do we need more information and advice on the child's needs from outside?
● The SENCO will be able to support you in the action you take. The SENCO works closely with the member of staff responsible for the child, and draws on the advice from outside specialists.
● The SENCO also ensures that the child and his or her parents/carers are consulted and kept informed.
● One of you (usually the class teacher) will need to draw up an IEP, incorporating specialist advice and arrange to review this regularly.
● Your role will then be to ensure that the child's IEP is incorporated within your curriculum planning for the *whole* class.
● The SENCO will also liaise with outside specialists, arrange for progress to be monitored and keep the headteacher informed.
● Sometimes School Action Plus will lead to a special support teacher having an input. Your role might become one of co-ordinating their support so that the child is included in the curriculum.

Finding out more
Send for catalogues on supporting many kinds of SEN in your classroom from: David Fulton Publishers, The Chiswick Centre, 414 Chiswick High Road, London W4 5TF, www.fultonpublishers.co.uk National Association for Special Educational Needs (NASEN), 4–5 Amber Business Village, Amber Close, Amington, Tamworth, Staffordshire B77 4RP. www.nasen.org.uk.

WORKING WITH CARERS
● Parents and carers should always be part of the decision to refer their child to an outside agency. In most cases, they need to give their express consent.
● If they are unhappy about this, explain that you wish to do everything that is best for their child and, to do this, *you yourself* need further advice from an outside professional.

MAKING LINKS
● Contact your LEA support service or SEN section for information on your local support services.
● Contact the school nurse or child health clinic for information on NHS professionals who support school children in the community.
● See also the pages on Code of Practice for SEN (page 20), IEPs (page 36) and School Action (page 47).

School phobia

What you need to know

● School phobia is an anxiety-related disorder and leads to the child finding it impossible to come into school because of extreme levels of fear and anxiety. It is more common in adolescent children.

● It is a complex response, which might be triggered by a number of different factors, and it needs careful assessment (usually by an outside professional) if it is to be distinguished from a simple refusal to go to school.

● If the child is refusing to come to school (even when parents or carers are encouraging them to), this might be related to a phobia or fear of travelling or meeting people, or it might be due to a fear of school. It might also be linked to a separation anxiety or there might be aspects of social withdrawal related to mental health difficulties such as depression.

How to help

● Keep a careful note of attendance and, whenever possible, make sure you record the reasons for absence and whether you were notified of this by the parents or carers.

● If you see a pattern of non-attendance emerging, gather more information from parents and carers and begin to make your own assessment of the situation (see above).

● Children who develop a fear of school often try to cope with it by avoiding the situation. Unfortunately, it is the opposite that will help.

● If you think a child is vulnerable, do all that you can in the early stages to establish what the child might be worried about and to take practical steps to overcome the problem.

● Develop 'buddy systems' and pastoral mentoring to support vulnerable children.

● Encourage parents and carers to send children back quickly after minor illnesses.

● Try to maintain some sort of attendance, even if it is just a short visit to the classroom at the end of the day or a stay until break-time. Step by small step is better than total avoidance.

● Suggest that the family seek further help, perhaps via the education social worker in the first instance.

● Provide a 'nurture corner' for troubled children to withdraw to if they feel in need of quiet personal space for a short time during the school day.

Finding out more
Helping Families with Troubled Children – A preventative approach by Carole Sutton (Wiley).

WORKING WITH CARERS
● If you are working with a 'separation anxiety', then you are likely to be dealing with an anxious parent or carer as well as an anxious child. Do what you can to boost parents'/carers' confidence and make them feel involved in their child's education.

MAKING LINKS
● The education social work service at your LEA is there to support you in attendance issues and in home–school liaison.
● See also Emotional difficulties (page 29) and Separation anxiety (page 55).

Self-esteem

What you need to know

● It is possible to tell when a child suffers from low self esteem. Quite often you will notice certain characteristics and patterns of behaviour, though they are not a fixed rule.

● Of course, we all feel 'up' and 'down' on particular days depending on recent events, our general sense of well-being, our health and our moods. Children, too, have their 'good days' and their 'bad days'.

● Children who have low self-esteem often have a strong need for reassurance and may appear to feel insecure or prickly.

● Children with low self-esteem have a low opinion of themselves, little faith in their own capabilities and easily become tearful when things go wrong. They are often reluctant to express their opinions and find it hard to make decisions.

● Sometimes they tend to overreact to failure, find it hard to accept correction and are oversensitive to criticism.

● Sometimes they seem to feel safer if they take control, and you might find that they are frequently testing boundaries or dominating other children's learning and play. They might have a tendency to hurt or bully others.

How to help

● Use a warm, positive approach with each child and invest individual time in your relationship. A key worker system for vulnerable children in which one member of staff is responsible for befriending and supporting certain children can be helpful.

● Positive approaches to managing difficult behaviour help to ensure that the child's self-esteem remains intact.

● Children who are nagged constantly with 'don't...' and 'no', tend to stop listening or trying after a while, and come to see themselves as naughty. Even if the nagging occurs at home, the reaction can spill over into the classroom.

● Children whose appropriate behaviour is noticed and praised, are more likely to repeat the behaviours that are attracting your admiration and to see themselves as helpful and kind.

● Confidence and learning seem to be bound together. If a child tries something new and fails, their self-esteem and self-confidence become lower and they are less likely to try again.

Finding out more
The Emotional Literacy Handbook – Promoting Whole School Strategies by James Park, Alice Haddon and Harriet Goodman (David Fulton).

WORKING WITH CARERS
● Children who have warm, affectionate relationships with their parents or carers generally develop high self-esteem and a positive image of themselves.
● Help parents/carers tune into their child and enjoy each other's company more by setting homework tasks in which the child can 'show off' what he or she has learned at school.
● Try to convey the message that children who are encouraged rather than criticised or pressured actually do better at school.

MAKING LINKS
● Contact your local LEA advisory service for training on circle time approaches – these are a helpful way to boost self-esteem.
● See also the pages on Behaviour difficulties (page 15) and Emotional literacy (page 30).

Semantic pragmatic difficulties

What you need to know

● Some children develop speech and language reasonably well, but have subtle difficulties in understanding the social nature of language and conversation.

● Children with 'semantic and pragmatic' language difficulties have difficulties both in the understanding of abstract language and in the social use of language.

● They might stick to topics of intense interest, not wait for gaps in a conversation before cutting in, use poor eye contact, and become quickly distressed if they cannot handle social situations (like asking to go to the toilet or asking for help from a supply teacher).

● They tend to take a long time to settle in a new class until the adults and surroundings are very familiar.

● Usually, their understanding of abstract words is very poor (for example 'quiet', 'kind', 'unusual'), though their understanding of concrete and literal words can be excellent.

● Imaginative play and creative thinking is often missing or limited.

● They may find it hard to see another person's point of view and can therefore behave antisocially at times.

● These difficulties are similar to those on the autistic continuum but often improve as their language and literacy skills develop.

How to help

● Sometimes these children need plenty of opportunity to hear language, listen to you talking and explaining, and feel excited enough by their learning to want to talk about it. Keep your language simple and emphasise key topic words, explaining new words carefully.

● Help these children see the other child's point of view and maintain a flow to their interaction. Teach conversation skills by explaining how close the child should stand, where the child should look and how to listen as well as to speak.

● Explain ways that the child can focus the listener on their subject by introducing the topic first and taking into account whether the listener understands what they are talking about.

● Use a light touch or pre-agreed hand signal to make sure the child is looking at you as you talk to them in class.

● Use a simple timetable to let them know what will happen next during your lessons.

● Always show these children what to do as well as telling them.

● Check regularly that the child comprehends what they are reading and explain any unknown vocabulary.

Finding out more

Contact the Association for All Speech Impaired Children (AFASIC): 2nd Floor, 50–52 Great Sutton Street, London EC1V 0DJ, 0207 490 9410, www.afasic.org.uk.

WORKING WITH CARERS

● Invest time in talking to parents and carers about their child. This will help you put any unusual behaviour into context and prevent your seeing it as naughty.

MAKING LINKS

● Contact any speech and language therapist who might be involved so that you can link in with their approaches. Parents/carers might be able to help you keep in touch through a regular notebook.

● See also the pages on Asperger's Syndrome (page 11), autistic spectrum difficulties (page 14) and Speech and language difficulties (page 57).

SEN

What you need to know

● If you have not worked with children who have SEN before, you might be unsure what the term means. It is important to see SEN not as something 'within the child' that can be seen, but as the way in which the child is learning and how they respond to teaching.

● Though it might be obvious that a child has SEN because of a particular disability, most children with SEN are experiencing learning difficulties for a wider range of reasons and without any 'diagnosis' as such.

● It is best to make a pragmatic decision as to whether a child has SEN based on what the child is doing, what you have tried and what seems to be effective.

● You may find that there are some children in your group who seem to need *additional* or *different* approaches to help them play and develop, even after they have had time to settle in your class and you have tried all your usual approaches. These are the children who are said to have 'special educational needs' or 'SEN'.

● Sometimes you know the reasons – perhaps a child has grown up with a condition that affects their development such as cerebral palsy (page 17), or perhaps they are delayed in their ability to speak and communicate because of autism (page 13). However, you do not need a medical label in order to be able to help.

● In other words, these children do not have special needs because they look different, because they have a particular label or because they behave in an unusual way. They have special needs because they fail to make acceptable progress even when you have tried all your usual approaches.

● The SEN Code of Practice gives you guidance on how to meet SEN in your school (page 19) and the school's SENCO (page 53) is there to support you in your work with children who have SEN.

How to help

● Allow all children time to settle in and respond to your usual approaches for differentiation before you assume they have SEN.

● Start by gathering information through observation and record keeping. You will be monitoring the progress of all the children so your system for monitoring a child who has SEN can arise naturally from your existing approaches, but be in much more detail.

● Use diary records, photographs, SAT scores, teacher assessments and examples of the child's work and creations to build up a dossier of the child's interests, strengths, progress and areas of need.

● Always plan a simple intervention and assess progress before assuming that the child is not learning effectively – this is a form of 'dynamic assessment'.

Finding out more

See the *Special Needs Handbook* from this series.

WORKING WITH CARERS

● Look for methods of assessment and observation that involve what is happening at home as well and which involve families.

MAKING LINKS

● Sometimes children join your group with a disability or special need already identified. If so, there should be information available to you from parents/carers and professionals.

● See also Learning difficulties (page 39), Code of Practice (page 19), School Action/Plus (pages 47–48) and SENCO (page 53).

SENCO

What you need to know
● The importance of having a special educational needs co-ordinator in every school has been stated clearly in government guidance.
● While the headteacher and SENCO are there to advise and support colleagues, provision for children with special educational needs is the responsibility of all the teachers in the school and particularly class teachers.
● The SENCO works with heads and senior staff to put together, monitor and review the SEN policy for the school (page 54).
● The main responsibility of the SENCO is to work with everyone to ensure that SEN policy works effectively and inclusively in each class.

How to help
● Find out from the SENCO what the procedures are in your school for working with and including disabled children and those with other forms of SEN. Make sure that you have a copy of the SEN policy for the school and understand how you fit into this.
● Ask the SENCO for advice about how to identify, support and monitor these children's needs. If a child has an unusual pattern of learning which the SENCO has not worked with before, then they should be able to find out more information for you.
● If you feel that a child might have SEN, discuss this with the SENCO and decide whether that child's name should be added to your SEN register or equivalent recording system.
● There are likely to be recording systems for the school that you will need to comply with. Usually there is a form for you to complete if you have an initial concern about a child's progress, and further record forms to help you plan and monitor the IEP.
● Talk to the SENCO if you feel you need more information on any child with SEN. There is likely to be a confidential file with information and correspondence on children with SEN and it might be appropriate for you to have access.
● The SENCO should be able to support you in differentiating the curriculum and in setting appropriate targets for meeting individual children's needs and entitlements through an IEP (page 36).

Finding out more
How to survive and succeed as a SENCO in the primary school by Veronica Birkett (LDA).

WORKING WITH CARERS
● Although it may not be the SENCO's direct responsibility to liaise with every individual parent or carer of a child with SEN, he or she must support staff to make sure this happens smoothly and effectively.
● The SENCO should also be responsible for supporting staff in meetings or reviews with parents/ carers, and in setting appropriate targets, review dates and times.

MAKING LINKS
● The SENCO can keep you in touch with any national or local developments on provision for children with SEN, arrange training for you and make links with outside agencies.
● See also 'SEN policy' (page 54).

SEN policy

What you need to know

● Each school should have an SEN policy that is monitored and revised regularly. It is also inspected regularly by OFSTED.

● It is the SENCO's responsibility to work with the team to produce a written SEN policy and make sure it is cross-referenced to other relevant policies such as the admissions policy and the equal opportunities policy.

● The policy should begin with a short summary of the beliefs shared by staff regarding pupils with SEN.

● The policy should then show how staff:
- ensure the entitlement for all children to the curriculum,
- monitor, record and evaluate all children's progress,
- identify, assess and review SEN,
- provide additional resources and support for children with SEN.

● It goes on to show how the staff work with parents/carers and agencies and details the training and expertise already existing.

How to help

● Make sure that you have read and are familiar with your school's SEN policy.

● Remember that it is each staff member's responsibility to implement the policy, so speak to the SENCO if you are not sure what you should be doing.

● You should have an IEP in place for each child with SEN and you should be clear how you are going to put this into practice and what progress you are looking for.

● Think about how effective the policy is for the children you work with and for your own practice. Take an active part in feeding this back to the SENCO ready for the regular policy review.

● Inform the SENCO of any training or particular experience you have had in SEN so that this can appear in the policy.

● You should find recent and relevant information in the SEN policy about the support services available to you and the way in which your school would access this. Help to keep this up-to-date in the light of your experience.

● Class teachers are ideally placed to talk with children with SEN about their SEN and the help they are receiving. In this way, you can contribute the voices of the children to the regular SEN policy review.

Finding out more

The SENCO Handbook – Working within a whole-school approach by Elizabeth Cowne (David Fulton Publishers).

WORKING WITH CARERS

● The SEN policy should show how staff share the responsibility for meeting SEN with parents/carers, how they share information and how they respond to parental concerns.

● Listen to what parents/carers say about the SEN provision in your school and feed this back to the SENCO for the policy review.

MAKING LINKS

● The SEN policy should also show how staff work with LEAs, health services, social services and other agencies on any matter to do with the school's SEN work.

● See also the *Special Needs Handbook* by Hannah Mortimer (Scholastic) from this series for detailed information about how the SEN policy can work in a primary school.

Separation anxiety

What you need to know

● It is absolutely normal for a young child to be anxious and mildly distressed when they first separate from a parent and carer and come into school. It is far more unusual for an older child (aged six or over) to continue to be distressed. Separation anxiety can also develop suddenly, for example after a family breakdown, bereavement or other major event or trauma in the child's life, which can affect older children.

● Each child is individual in this respect – many (often those with older siblings) separate and settle happily from the very first day.

● A few children continue to be distressed on separation and cannot be consoled or become 'frozen' and isolated in school. These children are sometimes said to have a 'separation anxiety'.

● Sometimes separation anxiety is linked to other unusual behaviours such as selective mutism in which the child will only speak in certain situations (for example to other children but not to the teacher).

How to help

● Whenever possible, plan visits to school for new starters and their parents and carers before a new starter joins your class.

● If you know that a new starter has a history of being highly anxious, arrange a home visit so that the child can begin to form an attachment with you before they join your class.

● Arrange for a 'buddy' or key-worker to greet and distract the child as he or she arrives, calmly but confidently.

● Occasionally, it might be appropriate to use a cuddly or themed toy for security. For example, one seven-year-old was supported positively by a figure of Gandalf from *Lord of the Rings* after his foster placement broke down. In time, the child may be happy to place it on a special shelf to 'watch' or to use it to express ideas and feelings when he or she is feeling overwhelmed.

● Plan 'transfer objects' when a child first arrives – something the child has brought from home to show you perhaps. This eases the transfer from home to school. Allow the child to arrive a little early or a little late if this helps too.

● It is fine to plan for a parent or carer to come in with a highly anxious child for a little while, but make this part of a planned progression towards helping the child become more emotionally independent. At that stage, be tough and show that you expect the parent to leave.

Finding out more

The book *Activities for including children with behavioural difficulties* from this series also covers emotional difficulties.

WORKING WITH CARERS

● If a child is so distressed that the education is significantly disrupted, talk to parents/carers about seeking a referral though the GP to the local Child and Adolescent Mental Health Service. Alternatively, talk to the education social worker.

● Give parents/carers ideas about 'letting go' of their child in situations outside of school, such as through joining out-of-school clubs and activities.

MAKING LINKS

● Talk with the education social worker if you are very concerned. He or she might be able to work with the family to support a happier pattern of attendance.

Specific learning difficulties

What you need to know

● Some children seem to have a specific difficulty in reading, writing, or calculating despite being of average intelligence and despite managing other aspects of their learning well. These children are sometimes said to have a 'specific learning difficulty'.

● It is called 'specific' because the difficulty is greater than you might expect, given the child's obvious intelligence and ability. Professionals sometimes use labels to describe different forms of specific learning difficulty. Dyslexia is the most familiar. There is also developmental co-ordination disorder (formerly referred to as developmental dyspraxia), number blindness (dyscalculia) and a writing difficulty called dysgraphia.

● However, the use of labels makes the whole subject seem simpler than it is. In fact, specific learning difficulties are usually caused by a complex interaction of strengths, weaknesses and learning experiences and there is overlap between different areas.

● Some teachers use the words 'specific learning difficulty' and 'dyslexia' to mean the same thing. It is important to know that there are many types of specific learning difficulty all related although individual to the child concerned.

● In order to plan the best ways of helping, you need to know what the specific learning difficulty actually means to the child – perhaps they have a weak memory for what they see or hear, or perhaps they cannot distinguish the sounds within words.

How to help

● Don't be alarmed when children 'mirror write' – this is common up to age six, especially in children with mixed handedness.

● Develop and improve the child's language skills and vocabulary use in oral situations.

● Introduce sound and rhyming activities at an early stage.

● Practise sequencing tasks, for example arranging pictures of a simple story or recounting simple experiences in chronological order.

● Introduce a phonic approach (learning letter sounds) at an early age, for example, using the *Jolly Phonics* series from Jolly Learning.

● Use game-like approaches to inspire motivation and confidence when introducing literacy and numeracy skills at Key Stage 1.

● Use multi-sensory approaches to learning in which the child sees, hears, feels and manipulates. Make sure that activities appeal to all types of learners – the visual, the auditory and the kinaesthetic.

● Teach looking and listening skills as part of building up concentration and attention.

● Use music and songs to teach sequences such as counting, days of the week or the alphabet.

Finding out more

Specific Learning Difficulties by Dorothy Smith (NASEN).

WORKING WITH CARERS

● Specific learning difficulties often run in families and taking a relevant family history can help you identify if a child might be at risk.

MAKING LINKS

● Contact the LEA learning support service for advice and information. See also the pages on Dyslexia and DCD/dsypraxia (page 22).

Speech and language difficulties

What you need to know

● Some children's speech and language development is delayed, but nevertheless progressing along normal lines. Perhaps these children are delayed in other areas of their development as well and the language delay is just one part of this immaturity.

● Children might lack the ability to make certain sounds or to co-ordinate them in the required sequence. These may be described as having 'dyspraxic', 'dysarthric' or 'articulation' difficulties.

● Some children can't speak clearly, or their language remains like a telegram. For others there is a specific language disorder which means that their brains are working in a different way from most other children and they would benefit from specialist therapy.

● *Understanding* of language (*receptive* language) is usually affected as well as *use* of language (*expressive* language).

● Children who have had speech and language difficulties earlier in their lives may continue to have difficulties in word finding, vocabulary or comprehension later in their school careers. There is also a higher likelihood of specific learning difficulties.

How to help

● Start by assessing the child's speech and language by observing their interactions, by recording extracts of their language and understanding and by taking recordings.

● Make sure that each child's hearing has been checked and contact the school nurse if you are concerned.

● Provide plenty of opportunities for developing concepts – provide the child with experiences of concepts in mathematics and science such as 'empty', 'lots', 'long', so that the child can make links in thinking and learn to generalise the word to new situations.

● Time can be a particularly hard concept for the child with receptive language difficulties; use visual timetables and concrete examples ('*When* you finished this page, *then* it is break time').

● Keep your language simple and clear, emphasising key words and showing children what to do as well as telling them.

● Try not to overload these children with language – they can become quickly frustrated if you fire long questions at them or give lengthy explanations and may 'switch off' from what you are saying.

● For severely affected children, ensure you have assessed how they make their needs known so that you can respond appropriately.

● Monitor progress in English especially carefully.

Finding out more

AFASIC, 2nd Floor, 50–52 Great Sutton Street, London EC1V 0DJ, 0207 490 9410, www.afasic.org.uk.

WORKING WITH CARERS

● Ask parents or carers to keep a home–school–therapy diary so that you can follow through any speech and language therapy advice with the child.

MAKING LINKS

● Speech and Language therapists provide specialist assessment of all aspects of children's speech, language and communication and can work with families and schools on the best ways to help. Contact the parents/carers or school nurse if you feel a referral might be necessary.

● See also the pages on Dyslexia (page 27) Semantic pragmatic difficulties (page 51), Specific learning difficulties (page 56) and Stammering (page 59).

Spina bifida and hydrocephalus

What you need to know

● The condition of spina bifida is present from birth and affects the child's physical and neurological development.

● Spina bifida is a fault in the spinal column in which one of the vertebrae (or bones which form the backbone) fails to form properly, leaving a gap or split.

● It happens very early in pregnancy, and the spinal cord may not develop properly, forming a cyst or protrusion outside the spine.

● The amount of disability depends on how greatly the spinal cord is affected, where the bifida is, and the amount of nerve damage.

● Often there is paralysis below the fault, with incontinence and a difficulty or lack of walking.

● Inevitably these children may have difficulties in spatial awareness if they have lacked the usual early learning experiences.

How to help

● Talk to parents/carers about what the condition means for their particular child. How much help is needed for him or her move around, reach, and stay clean and dry?

● If there is a wheelchair, special seating or standing frames, ask parents/carers for a demonstration so that you can make any adjustments necessary during the time at school.

● Take pains to find out about a child's strengths and interests so that you make sure to allow him or her to learn independently whenever possible, rather than shadowing the child with your care and concern. Children can soon let you know when they need your help if you are always available and responsive.

● Make sure your tables, work surfaces and easels are at the right height for any special seats or buggies, and try to store your craft activities and learning resources at a level that allows all your children to make choices and reach for them.

● Plan PE activities in a way that allows wheelchair users or non-ambulant children to participate as fully as possible.

● Monitor skills in design and technology, in art and design and in spatial aspects of mathematics in case the child needs extra explanation or a more multi-sensory teaching approach.

Finding out more

The Association for Spina Bifida and Hydrocephalus, ASBAH House, 42 Park Road, Peterborough PE1 2UQ, 01733 555988, www.asbah.org.

WORKING WITH CARERS

● Allow parents/ carers to show you routines or equipment so that you become confident in taking over from them.

● Make sure your spaces are accessible.

● Encourage older children to be responsible for their own care and independence.

● Ask parents/carers if there is anything you need to know about risk of infection – for example, if there are chest infections in school, will they need to arrange preventative medication?

MAKING LINKS

● If you find that the child is missing out on an activity because of being in the wrong position or having the wrong equipment, contact the occupational therapist for ideas.

● See also the pages on Disability Act (page 25), Independence training (page 36) and Physical difficulties (page 45).

Stammering

What you need to know

● Most young children pass through a stage when they begin to stammer. They find themselves full of exciting ideas but do not have the language to express them. When the brain thinks of ideas faster than words can articulate them, children begin to stammer and stutter as if to buy time for themselves. This is absolutely normal.

● Some children get stuck in this phase. They frequently stammer on words and particularly on *parts* of words. For many of these children, this seems to get worse for them at times when they feel rushed or anxious, but for other children, there is no pattern to this at all.

● Many people who stammer come to learn that there are certain sounds or words they cannot say and learn to select easier ways of saying things. This can add 'thinking' time when you are working with the child in an oral situation.

● Researchers feel there may be several different causes to stammering and it is not caused by anxiety alone. Most children who stammer get over their difficulties, but a few do not.

● If children become 'stuck' in a stammering phase, they need speech and language therapy.

● Children who stammer will find aspects of speaking and listening challenging and need flexible approaches for presenting to a large group. They usually find public speaking embarrassing and prefer visual presentation.

How to help

● Never hurry the children's speech if they are keen to tell you something. Listen patiently to what they are saying, and try very hard not to interrupt or complete their thoughts for them.

● Keep looking at the child as you listen, and reply slowly and unhurriedly after a second or two's pause; this slows the whole exchange down to a more relaxed tempo.

● Try to spend more time than usual talking with that child in a relaxed situation. Children who stammer find it easiest to talk about things of personal interest to them, and most difficult when you expect them to answer questions in front of everybody.

● If it causes difficulties, don't insist on a spoken answer if you take a register. Ask the child to nod or give a thumbs up signal instead.

● If the child has got a hand up during a class discussion, let them answer fairly soon to prevent any anxiety building up.

● Some children find drama easy as they are in role rather than speaking for themselves. For others, this causes too much anxiety.

● Music can be excellent for encouraging participation, as many people who stammer find they can sing words they cannot speak.

Finding out more

The British Stammering Association is based at 15 Old Ford Road, London E2 9PJ (www.stammering.org).

WORKING WITH CARERS

● Encourage parents and carers to make talking and conversation as fun as they can so that their child joins in fully despite any difficulties. This way you can all prevent a child becoming self conscious about a stammer.

MAKING LINKS

● Your local NHS Speech and Language Therapy Services is involved in helping families identify children who stammer and can provide specialist help and advice. See also the page on Speech and language difficulties (page 57).

SPECIAL NEEDS in the primary years

Statement of SEN

What you need to know
● For a very few children (about 2%), the help provided by School Action Plus (page 48) will still not ensure satisfactory progress.
● The SENCO, external professional and parents/carers may then ask the LEA to consider carrying out a statutory assessment of the child's SEN.
● The LEA must decide quickly whether it has the evidence that a statutory assessment is necessary. It is then responsible for co-ordinating the assessment and will call for the various reports that it requires, from the class teacher, support teacher, an educational psychologist, a doctor, and social services if involved. It will also ask parents or carers to submit their own views and 'evidence'.
● The whole procedure must not take longer than six months unless there are exceptional circumstances (listed in the Code of Practice).
● The statutory assessment may or may not lead to a 'statement' of SEN. This states what the special needs are, what provision will be made for them, how the needs will be monitored, and where the child will be placed.
● Sometimes it is necessary for the LEA to write a 'note in lieu of statement' instead, which is similar to a formalised IEP to be implemented and monitored by the school.
● When a school is named on the statement, the LEA will ask the SENCO to call regular (usually annual) reviews to monitor whether the child's needs are being met.

How to help
● Keep all copies of IEPs and review meetings – you may need these to attach as evidence to any request for a statutory assessment.
● During a statutory assessment, parents/carers will receive a number of formal letters from the LEA. The LEA is required by law to send these, and it is often helpful if the class teacher or SENCO can reassure parents/carers about their contents and put them in touch with the independent parental supporter or parent partnership officer (page 43) if they need explanations or have concerns or queries.
● If you are approached for a report, then you will be given a strict time for returning it to the LEA. You might also attach samples of the child's work or behavioural observations that you have made.
● Remember that your report will be circulated to parents/carers and all professionals involved. It is helpful to discuss it with parents/carers first.

Finding out more
Read the free leaflet 'Assessments and Statements' from CSIE (Centre for Studies in Inclusive Education) available from New Redland, Frenchay Campus, Coldharbour Lane, Bristol, BS16 1QU. A list of further publications is available at http://inclusion.uwe.ac.uk.

WORKING WITH CARERS
● Parents/carers have various rights of appeal to an SEN Tribunal if they are not happy with the statutory assessment procedures or the statement, and these are fully covered in the SEN Code of Practice.

MAKING LINKS
● Talk to your SENCO, LEA support teacher or educational psychologist for information and advice.
● See also the pages on Code of Practice for SEN (page 19) and Parent supporters (page 43).

Trauma

What you need to know

● A trauma can be any distressing event. Trauma causes an extreme stress reaction that can take its time to settle. The stress reaction is a normal reaction to an abnormal event.

● Each child goes through his or her own process of readjusting to a traumatic event. Some children may display intense emotions, and others may seem frozen or behave as if nothing was different. All are normal responses. Some will behave as if they were younger, wanting constant reassurance, thumb sucking or throwing tantrums.

● Others may appear pre-occupied and find it hard to concentrate.

● Just because a child has been through a trauma does not mean they need professional help. It is usually best to provide support through family, teachers and close friends (with outside professional advice if necessary) rather than new professionals. However, sometimes children can become 'stuck' in their recovery process.

● These children may go on to need therapeutic help from a counsellor or child psychologist.

How to help

● Provide a 'secure base' for the child through their period of readjustment – perhaps a quiet space where they can withdraw too if they need to. Spend more time with the child and let him or her become more dependent on you for a while. The need for constant reassurance might be there for several months and the need for occasional 'extra' reassurance can last beyond a year.

● Provide learning experiences to help relieve tension. Younger children find it easiest to share their feelings and ideas through play than words. Provide imaginative play, small-world play, and picture books that help to make sense of their situation. Older children find it helpful to talk, draw and write about their experiences or feelings.

● Stick to familiar routines. Being with familiar people in a familiar and secure classroom helps children to realise that their basic security and their sense of who they are can still carry on.

● Arrange a regular one-to-one pastoral session so that you have a regular opportunity to talk to the child about how he or she is feeling.

● Discreetly inform other staff that the child has suffered a trauma, so that they understand why the child might appear 'different'.

Finding out more

Barnardo's produce the 'Memory Store' and 'Memory Book' for children facing separation, loss and bereavement. Write to: Barnardo's Child Care Publications, Barnardo's Trading Estate, Paycocke Road, Basildon, Essex. SS14 3DR or contact via their website, www.barnardos.org.uk. The Child Bereavement Trust can be contacted at: Aston House, West Wycombe, High Wycombe, Buckinghamshire. HP14 3AG. Send for their information pack. Alternatively, visit www.childbereavement.org.uk, for information.

WORKING WITH CARERS

● Don't be afraid to discuss the child's emotional progress.

● Use your basic knowledge of reactions to trauma to reassure them that things do take time to readjust.

MAKING LINKS

● If you are concerned that the child's reactions are not 'moving on', discuss this with the SENCO, education social worker or educational psychologist.

● See also 'Bereavement' (page 15), 'Emotional difficulties' (page 29) and 'Play therapy' (page 46).

Visual impairment

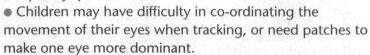

What you need to know

● Some children have difficulty in seeing things clearly unless they are close up and well lit. They are severely near-sighted or 'myopic'.
● Some can only see clearly at a distance. They may be severely far-sighted or 'presbyopic'.

● Children may have difficulty in co-ordinating the movement of their eyes when tracking, or need patches to make one eye more dominant.
● Some children cannot identify between different colours. Colour-blindness can take different forms.
● Some children have patches of blindness or even tunnel vision, which restricts their field of vision.
● Some children's sight is so restricted that they are effectively blind; about 5% of children with visual impairment go on to use Braille for reading and writing.

How to help

● Choose brightly coloured resources, posters and illustrations that attract visual attention.
● Make sure your learning spaces are well lit and free from unnecessary clutter and obstacles.
● Have well-defined areas for putting away your resources and materials so that a child with visual difficulties can always find them.
● Have well-defined areas for your large construction equipment, for PE apparatus and for practical activity, so that children with poor sight are not bumped into in the quieter areas.
● Use carpets, curtains and soft furnishings to absorb sound and therefore make sounds easier to hear and to locate.
● Be aware that children whose vision is restricted (even spectacles restrict the range of vision) may not see you approach. Approach from the front if you can, and say the child's name so that they can identify you from your voice. Ask other children to do the same.
● Sit children with near-sight close to the front at group time and for plenary discussion times.
● Look for large-print books from your local library. If necessary, consider a sloping desktop and magnifying apparatus for close study work.
● Ask the specialist support teacher whether you should be considering close-circuit TV for practical work in science and design and technology. This allows practical demonstrations by the teacher to be relayed via a TV monitor to the pupil, thereby enabling him or her to see what is happening at a distance.
● Enlarge photocopies and use large point sizes when word-processing.

Finding out more

The RNIB can be contacted at: Royal National Institute of the Blind, 105 Judd Street, London, WC1H 9NE, www.rnib.org.

WORKING WITH CARERS
● Talk through your typical school day and establish where and when the child might need supporting. Negotiate the best way of encouraging maximum independence and responsibility in learning and care.

MAKING LINKS
● Most LEAs have support teachers for children with visual impairment who can advise you on the implications of the child's condition, on access to Braille and on specialist equipment.
● See also the entries on Disability Act (page 25) and Inclusion (page 37).

USEFUL CONTACTS

NATIONAL ORGANISATIONS

● **Alliance for Inclusive Education,** Unit 2, 70 South Lambeth Road, London SE8 1RL Tel: 020 7735 5277, www.allfie.org.uk.
– Campaigns to end compulsory segregation of children with special education needs within the education system.

● **Barnardo's**, Tanners Lane, Barkingside, Ilford, Essex, IG6 1QG, Tel: 020 8550 8822, www.barnardos.org.uk.
– Provides care and support for children in need and their families, with projects throughout the UK, and distributes usful publications and resources.

● **The Child Psychotherapy Trust**, Star House, 104-108 Grafton Road, London NW5 4BD, www.childpsychotherapytrust.org.uk.
– Produces several 'Understanding Childhood' leaflets covering emotional and mental health issues – send for a catalogue.

● **Children in Scotland** (training and information on services), 5 Shandwick Place, Princes House, Edinburgh EH2 4RG. Tel: 0131 2288484, www.childreninscotland.org.uk.
– Holds courses in SEN.

● **Children's Society**, Edward Rudolf House, Margery Street, London, WC1X 0JL, Tel: 0845 300 11 28 www.the-childrens-society.org.uk.
– Works with children in need and their families. Runs several family centres and parenting projects.

● **The Department for Education and Skills** (DfES) 08700 000 22 88, www.dfes.gov.uk.
– Parent information and government advice and circulars, including the SEN Code of Practice and *Removing Barriers to Achievement*.

● **I CAN Training Centre**, 4 Dyers Building, Holborn, London EC1N 2QP, Tel: 0870 0104066 www.ican.org.uk.
– Holds day courses for those working with language-impaired children.

● **Makaton Vocabulary Development Project**: 31, Firwood Drive, Camberley, Surrey. GU15 3QD, Tel:0127 661390, www.makaton.org.
– Information about Makaton sign vocabulary and training.

● **National Association for Special Educational Needs**, NASEN House, 4/5 Amber Business Village, Amber Close, Amington, Tamworth, Staffordshire, B77 4RP Tel: 01827 311500 Website: www.nasen.org.uk.
– Professional association with a database of relevant courses for those wishing to train in SEN; also runs training courses itself.

● **National Children's Bureau**, 8 Wakley Street, London EC1V 7QE Tel: 020 7843 6000, www.ncb.org.uk.
– A multidisciplinary organisation concerned with the promotion of the interests of all children and young people. Involved in research, policy and practice development, and consultancy.

● **National Council of Voluntary Child Care Organisations**, Unit 4, Pride Court, 80–82 White Lion Street, London, N1 9PF Tel: 020 7833 3319, www.ncvcco.org.
– Umbrella group for voluntary organisations dealing with children. Maximising the voluntary sector's contribution to the provision of services.

● **National Society for the Prevention of Cruelty to Children** (NSPCC) , Weston House, 42 Curtain Road, London, EC2A 3NH. Tel: 020 78252500, www.nspcc.org
– Provides training on SEN, child protection and family work.

RESOURCES

● **Acorn Educational Ltd**, 32 Queen Eleanor Road, Geddington, Kettering, Northants. NN14 1AY. Tel 01536 400212, www.acorneducational.co.uk.
– Supplies equipment and resources for special needs.

● **Being Yourself**, The Old Bakery, Charlton House, Dour Street, Dover, CT16 1ED. www.smallwood.co.uk.
– Hand puppets and therapeutic games for professionals working to improve mental wellbeing and emotional literacy in children.

● **CSIE** (Centre for Studies on Inclusive Education) New Redland, Frenchay Campus, Coldharbour Lane, Bristol BS16 1QU, http://inclusion.uwe.ac.uk.
– Publishes *Index for Inclusion: developing learning and participation in schools* by T. Booth, M. Ainscow, K. Black-Hawkins, M. Vaughan and L. Shaw.

● **Don Johnston Special Needs** 18/19 Clarendon Court, Calver Road, Winwick Quay, Warrington, WA2 8QP www.donjohnston.com.
– Produce a catalogue of resources of IT, early literacy intervention and building skills.

● **KCS**, FREEPOST, Southampton SO17 1YA, Tel: 023 8058 4314, www.keytools.com.
– Specialist tools for making computer equipment accessible to all children.

● **LDA** Primary and Special Needs catalogue is available from Duke Street, Wisbech, Cambridgeshire PE13 2AE, Tel. 01945 463441, www.ldalearning.com.
– Supplies *Circle Time Kit* by Jenny Mosley (puppets, rainstick, magician's cloak and many props for making circle time motivating.)

● **Lucky Duck Publishing Ltd**, Tel: 0117 973 2881, www.luckyduck.co.uk.
– Send for a catalogue of videos, SEN books and resources, especially for behavioural and emotional difficulties.

● **Magination Press** The Eurospan Group, 3 Henrietta Street, Covent Garden, London WC2E 8LU, www.maginationpress.com
– Specialises in books providing information and offering coping strategies for young children with personal or psychological concerns.

● **NES Arnold**, Novara House, Excelsior Road, Ashby Park, Ashby de la Zouch, LE65 1NG. Tel: 0845 120 45 25 www.nesarnold.co.uk.
– Publishes the *All About Me* materials by Sheila Wolfendale and can be used to involve children and parents in the assessment process.

● **Quality for Effective Development** (QEd), The Rom Building, Eastern Avenue, Lichfield, Staffs, WS13 6RN, www.qed.com.
– Publishes *Taking Part*, by Hannah Mortimer, which tells you how to talk to a child about statutory assessment.

● **SBS** (Step-by-step), Lee Fold, Hyde, Cheshire SK14 4LL. Tel 0845 3001089, www.sbs-educational.co.uk.
– Supplies toys for all special needs.